MW00641411

Trotsky's Lies

By Grover Furr

Erythros Press and Media, LLC
Corrected Edition August 2019

Trotsky's Lies
Corrected Edition, published August 2019

{A revised and updated edition of the Introduction, and Chapters
13-16 of Grover Furr, *Trotsky's 'Amalgams:' Trotsky's Lies, The
Moscow Trials As Evidence, The Dewey Commission*. Kettering, OH:
Erythrós Press & Media, LLC, 2015, 2016.}

Published by Erythrós Press and Media
PO Box 294994
Kettering, OH 45429-0994
media@erythrospress.com

© Grover Furr 2015, 2019

Published and printed with permission of the author, who as-
sumes all responsibility for the content herein.

Locally Assigned LC-type Call Number DK 254 .T6 F87122 2019

ISBN: 978-0-578-52104-6

198 pp. Includes index.

1. Trotsky, Leon, 1879-1940. 2. Revolutionaries - Russia- Biography. 3. Stalin, Joseph, 1878-1953. 4. Soviet Union – History – 1925-
1953. 5. Trials (Conspiracy).

Table of Contents

Acknowledgements and Dedication

Once again, I wish to express my gratitude to Kevin Prendergast, Arthur Hudson, and Siobhan McCarthy, the skilled and tireless Inter-Library Loan librarians at Harry S. Sprague Library, Montclair State University. Without their help my research would not be possible.

I would like to express my special thanks to my wonderful Moscow colleague Vladimir L'vovich Bobrov, for all his tireless and brilliant help during the past nineteen years of our research together.

My thanks to Effie Matlack, who did a superb job of proofreading this book and made many invaluable suggestions for changes and improvements.

* * * * *

I would like to recognize Montclair State University for giving me a sabbatical leave in the fall semester of 2015 for the purpose of working on this book.

* * * * *

Dedication

To Derek and Karla, Asia and Leona, my treasures.

Chapter 1. Trotsky's Lies

The justification for this book is twofold. First, during the past several decades a great many primary historical sources have been made available for the first time. Second, none of those who have written about Trotsky have made use of these sources.

These primary sources are important. They permit us to know a great deal more about Trotsky's activities during the 1930s than ever before. Yet despite this fact – or, perhaps, because of it – they have been almost entirely neglected.

These new primary sources are:

> * The Trotsky Archive at Houghton Library, Harvard University, open since January 2, 1980. In this book I refer to this as the "Harvard TA" or simply "TA."

> * A flood of documents from former Soviet archives published since the end of the Soviet Union in 1991 and continuing to this day.

Other collections of primary sources include the Trotsky-Sedov correspondence at the Hoover Institution, and documents made available but not published at various archives in Russia and elsewhere.

The documents from former Soviet archives have revolutionized our knowledge and understanding of Soviet history of the Stalin period, and thus of Soviet history as a whole. They permit us to see that much of what was written about Stalin and his era during Khrushchev's time, then during Gorbachev's tenure, and still today, is deliberately false – in plain language, lies.

The documents in the Harvard TA, and the research based on them by the late Pierre Broué, and by American historian Arch Getty, continue to be neglected by all writers on Trotsky even though –

or perhaps because – they demand of us a radically different view of Trotsky's activities during the 1930s and even before.

These primary sources now make it possible to check many of the fact-claims made by defendants in the Moscow Trials in the course of their testimony. For the first time we are able to objectively evaluate this important body of evidence by verifying some of the statements made in the Moscow Trials against independent sources.

This too has never been done. Since Nikita Khrushchev's "Secret Speech" to the XX Party Congress in February 1956 virtually all historians have dismissed the Moscow Trials testimony as false. The paradigm of the Moscow Trials has been that of innocent defendants forced to mouth false confessions to crimes they never committed by means of threats to themselves, against their families, etc. Their testimony has been universally rejected as fabricated, faked, "scripted" by the NKVD investigators, the prosecution, "Stalin."

But there has never been any *evidence* that the Moscow Trials testimony was fabricated. This has simply been asserted. This assertion has been "believed," accorded almost universal credence, because it has been voiced by seemingly diverse authorities: by Trotsky himself; by Soviet émigrés and dissidents who fled the USSR in the 1930s and thereafter; then by Khrushchev and by commissions and writers during his time; then by Mikhail Gorbachev and the commissions and writers sponsored by him; and since 1991 by both Russian and Western historians who claim to be drawing upon the newly-available documentation from former Soviet archives.

However, the truth is not constituted by any "consensus" of authorities. Nor is "credibility" a category of analysis. Whether a statement, fact-claim, etc. is "believed" has no bearing at all on whether it is true, no matter how many "authorities" affirm it. Only primary sources are evidence.

These newly-available primary sources – evidence – from the former Soviet archives and from the Harvard TA permit us to see for the first time that the history of the Soviet Union during the Stalin period, including the roles of Stalin and Trotsky, is very different – indeed, in many respects the diametrical opposite – from what we have been taught, and from what is still the "mainstream," "consensus" version.

* Thanks to these newly-available sources we can now see that Khrushchev, and then Gorbachev, lied about Soviet history of the Stalin period.

* We can also see now that Trotsky lied *too* — deliberately, as did Khrushchev and Gorbachev. Like them, Trotsky lied a lot.

I have written a number of books and articles about the lies perpetrated under the auspices of Khrushchev and Gorbachev, about anticommunist historians East and West who have drawn upon their lies, and about the new version of Soviet history that emerges from the newly-available archival sources. In *Trotsky's 'Amalgams'* (from which the present book is largely extracted), in *Leon Trotsky's Collaboration with Germany and Japan*, and in future volumes, I will identify and study some of Trotsky's lies and examine how this new evidence changes our understanding of Trotsky's activities and of Soviet history during the 1930s.

Trotsky's Lies

We owe, in great part, our introduction to the fact that Trotsky lied to a number of seminal works of research. First is the work of the late Pierre Broué, the foremost Trotskyist historian in the world during his time (Broué died in 2005). Second is the seminal article by J. Arch Getty, "Trotsky in Exile: The Founding of the Fourth International," published in *Soviet Studies* in January, 1986. Third is the brilliant article by Sven-Eric Holmström, "New Evidence Concerning the 'Hotel Bristol' Question in the First Moscow Trial of 1936," published in *Cultural Logic* for 2008. Inspired by the efforts of these researchers I have discovered some more lies by Trotsky.

Verifying the Moscow Trials Testimony

Part One of *Trotsky's 'Amalgams'* (excerpted and updated in *The Moscow Trials as Evidence*) consists of the process of verification of those fact-claims made by defendants in the three Moscow Trials that we can now check from other, independent sources. This project is important for understanding what Trotsky was doing during the 1930s.

According to the Moscow Trials testimony Trotsky, in the leadership of his clandestine followers within the USSR and in a political bloc with many other Oppositionists, was involved in the following conspiracies:

* To assassinate Stalin and other Soviet leaders (called "terror" or "individual terror" in Russian);

* To sabotage as much of the Soviet economy as possible, principally in industry, in mining, and in transportation;

* To conspire with commanders of the Soviet armed forces in order to promote a *coup d'état* against the Stalin regime;

* to take over leadership of the Soviet Union with the help of Hitler's Germany, militarist Japan, and other foreign powers at the price of making important economic concessions and of ceding parts of the Soviet Union to them, stopping support for the Comintern, and returning much or most of the economy back to private ownership.

Trotsky vigorously denied all of this. Especially since Khrushchev and Gorbachev, Trotsky's denials have been almost universally believed.

But the primary source evidence available to us today enables us to see that at the very least many, and indeed perhaps all, of the charges against Trotsky and the confessions made by the Moscow Trials defendants were true. *On the evidence, Trotsky's denials are lies.*

In *Trotsky's 'Amalgams', The Moscow Trials as Evidence,* the present book, and in future books I will examine those lies of Trotsky's that bear directly upon his conspiratorial activities and upon my verification of the Moscow Trials testimony. I do not mean to imply that these were all Trotsky was lying about. The more we study, the more lies of Trotsky's we discover.

Lenin's "Peppery Dishes" Statement

One example of a lie by Trotsky that does not bear directly upon his conspiracies or upon verification of the Moscow Trials testimony will serve to illustrate the fact that Trotsky lied a great deal. This is his claim that Lenin opposed Stalin's appointment as General Secretary of the Party because of his crude behavior towards others, which Trotsky called "peppery dishes."

I begin with what I believe to be the first time that Trotsky used this story. This was in his speech of October 23, 1927, to a combined meeting of the Plenum of the Central Committee and the Central Control Committee, called to consider his expulsion from the Party. Trotsky's "peppery dishes" statement is in **boldface** in the original, below:

The earliest version of Trotsky's "cook ... peppery dishes" story
***Pravda* November 2, 1927.**

Троцкий.—Через Октябрьскую революцию наша партия получила в свои руки могущественный аппарат принуждения, без которого немыслима пролетарская диктатура. Средоточием диктатуры является Центральный Комитет нашей партии. При Ленине, при ленинском Центральном Комитете организационный аппарат партии был подчинен революционной классовой политике мирового масштаба. Правда, Сталин, в качестве генерального секретаря, внушал Ленину опасения с самого начала. **«Сей повар будет готовить только острые блюда»**, — так говорил Ленин в тесном кругу в момент X съезда.[1]

---

[1] "Rech' tov. Trotskogo." *Pravda* November 2, 1927. Felix Kreisel has usefully put a photographic reproduction of this page of *Pravda* at http://web.mit.edu/fjk/www/images/Pravda/1927-11-02-4.pdf and transcribed the somewhat different version of Trotsky's speech from the MS in

Translated:

> Trotsky:—Through the October Revolution our Party re-
> ceived into its hands a powerful apparatus of compul-
> sion without which the proletarian dictatorship is un-
> thinkable. The concentration of the dictatorship is the
> Central Committee of our Party. In Lenin's time, in the
> time of Lenin's Central Committee, the organizational
> apparatus of the Party was subordinated to revolution-
> ary class politics of a global scale. True, Stalin in his ca-
> pacity of General Secretary instilled fear in Lenin from
> the very beginning. **"This cook will prepare only pep-
> pery** [literally: sharp – GF] **dishes,"** – so said Lenin to a
> small circle at the time of the X Party Congress.

In this first occurrence Trotsky clearly separated the "cook ... peppery dishes" story from Stalin's being made General Secretary.
Here Trotsky claims that Lenin made this remark "at the time of
the X Party Congress," which took place March 8 – 16, 1921. Stalin
was named to the post of General Secretary as a result of the XI
Congress held a year later, March 27 – April 2, 1922.

This would have been a good opportunity for Trotsky to name
others that also heard Lenin make this remark. It would, arguably,
have helped him, given his speech more impact, if he had done so.
But he did not. This makes us suspect that perhaps he *could* not do
so – that the story may be false.

It is difficult to prove that Lenin did *not* make this remark. Most
events do not leave a paper trail. For our purposes what is most
important here is that *even Trotsky does not claim that Lenin made
the remark in connection with Stalin's being made General Secretary.*

In February 1929, the same month he went into exile to Turkey,
Trotsky once again cited the "peppery dishes" story.

---

the Harvard TA at
http://web.mit.edu/fjk/www/Trotsky/sochineniia/1927/19271023.html

"This cook will prepare only **peppery dishes**," Lenin warned the party as early as 1922.

- "How Could This Happen?" February 25, 1929. WLT '29. p. 38.

Here Trotsky does not *explicitly* tie the story to Stalin's gaining the General Secretary post. But he does so *implicitly*, by shifting the date from 1921 to 1922, the year of the Eleventh Party Congress, the year Stalin was chosen as General Secretary.

Below are some of the citations of this statement in Trotsky's works. I do not claim that this is an exhaustive list.

Trotsky on "Peppery Dishes"

When at the Tenth Congress, two years after the death of Sverdlov, Zinoviev and others, not without a hidden thought of the struggle against me, supported the candidacy of Stalin for General Secretary – that is, placed him de jure in the position which Sverdlov had occupied de facto – Lenin spoke in a small circle against this plan, expressing his fear that "this cook will prepare only **peppery dishes**." That phrase alone, taken in connection with the character of Sverdlov, shows us the differences between the two types of organizers: the one tireless in smoothing over conflicts, easing the work of the Collegium, and the other a specialist in **peppery dishes** – not even afraid to spice them with actual poison.

- "On the Suppressed Testament of Lenin (December 1932)."
https://www.marxists.org/archive/trotsky/1932/12/lenin.htm

The necessity of removing the boss who was specializing in **peppery dishes** became clear to Lenin immediately after his return to work.

- Ibid.

In 1921, warning his most intimate comrades against electing Stalin as general secretary, Lenin said, "This cook will prepare only **peppery dishes**."

- "Some Results of the Stalin Amalgam" WLT '34-'35; also https://www.marxists.org/archive/trotsky/1935/01/a malgam.htm

From being the instrument of the revolution, the G.P.U. has become the instrument of the soviet aristocracy, the personal instrument of Stalin, about whom Lenin warned in 1922: "This cook will prepare only **peppery dishes**."

- "The Moscow 'Confessions'" 18 Dec. 1936

In 1922, when Stalin was first elected general secretary of the party, Lenin remarked warningly to a small circle: "This cook will give us only **peppery dishes**."

- "Is Stalin Weakening or the Soviets?" January 1932. WLT 1932 p. 38.

True to his evaluation of people and circumstances, Lenin in March 1922 spoke out decisively against the appointment of Stalin as general secretary ("that cook will make only **peppery dishes**")...

- "From the Archives," Sept. 1932 WLT 1932 p. 208.

Lenin saw the democratization of the administration as the most important task of the dictatorship. "Every cook must learn how to govern." The process that has taken place is quite the reverse. The number of administrators did not grow to include "every cook"; it constricted instead to a single chef, and at that a specialist in **peppery dishes** only.

- "Alarm Signal!" March 3, 1933. WLT 1932-33 p. 112.

In 1921, warning his most intimate comrades against electing Stalin as general secretary, Lenin said, "This cook will prepare only **peppery dishes**."

- "Some Results of the Stalin Amalgam." January 12, 1935. WLT 1934-35 p. 207.

You may remember that in 1921 Lenin had strongly advised the party against electing Stalin to the post of general secretary. "This cook" -- Lenin literally said – "will prepare only **spicy dishes**." In any case, Lenin could not at that moment have had the slightest idea of just how spicy this cook's dishes would be.[2]

- "Stalin Is Not Everything." August 23, 1936. WLT 1935-36 p. 411.

From being the instrument of the revolution, the GPU has become the instrument of the Soviet aristocracy, the personal instrument of Stalin, about whom Lenin warned in 1922: "This cook will prepare only **peppery dishes**."

- "Shame!" December 18, 1936. WLT 1935-36 p. 496.

It is astounding how persistent Zinoviev was, as he pulled Kamenev along, in preparing over a number of years his own tragic finale. If not for Zinoviev's initiative, Stalin would have hardly become the General Secretary of the Party. Zinoviev was bent on utilizing the episodic trade union discussion in the winter of 1920-21 for a further struggle against me. Stalin appeared to him -- and not without foundation -- the man most suitable for the behind-the-scenes work. It was during these very

---

[2] The Russian term is "ostrye bliuda," literally "sharp dishes," meaning "spicy" or "peppery." For some reason the translators used the term "spicy" here but "peppery" elsewhere.

days that Lenin, objecting to the appointment of Stalin as General Secretary, made his famous remark: "I do not advise it -- this cook will prepare only **peppery dishes**." What prophetic words!

- "Pages from Trotsky's Journal," 1936-1937.

In March 1921 Lenin had already given the advice not to choose Stalin as the general secretary since, as he put it, "This cook will prepare only **peppery dishes**." ... Thus the Kremlin "cook" came to the most peppery "dishes" in the form of the Moscow trials.

- "Statement to Journalists on the Dewey Verdict." December 13, 1937. WLT 1937-38 p. 98-9.

Lenin did not trust Stalin in 1921, when Zinoviev recommended him for the post of general secretary. Lenin gave the following warning: "I don't advise this. This cook will prepare only **peppery dishes**. "

- "Behind the Moscow Trials." March 3, 1938. WLT 1937-38 p. 203.

It was precisely at this point that Stalin brought into complete view the dangerous qualities which Lenin had warned against: rudeness, disloyalty, propensity to abuse power. The "cook of the Kremlin" had indeed prepared **the most peppery of dishes**.

- Ibid. p. 205.

... why it was precisely Stalin ("the cook of **peppery dishes**," according to Lenin's definition as far back as March 1921) who became head of the avid and conservative caste of usurpers of the revolution;

- "The Priests of Half-Truth." March 19, 1938. WLT 1937-38 p. 280.

Lenin proposed in his testament (January 1923) to remove Stalin from the post of general secretary of the
party, giving as his reasons Stalin's rudeness, disloyalty,
and tendency to abuse power. Two years earlier Lenin
warned: "This cook will prepare only **peppery dishes**."
No one in the party liked or respected Stalin... That is
why the cook of **peppery dishes** became the leader of
the totalitarian bureaucracy.

- "The Comintern and the GPU. The Attempted Assassination of May 24 and the Communist Party." WLT 1939-
40 p. 349 – 350.[3]

Trotsky made this claim many times. He vacillated between 1921
and 1922 as the year Lenin supposedly said it. Trotsky also vacillated over the question of to whom Lenin made this remark. Trotsky wrote "in a small circle," "his most intimate comrades," "his
famous remark," "warned the party," "to a small circle," "spoke out
decisively," "strongly advised the party," "gave the following warning."

Trotsky always claimed that others besides himself had heard
Lenin make this remark. His accounts differ significantly about
who and how many those people were. He never specifically name
anybody but himself. In addition, only Trotsky records it, no one
else. These considerations might provide reason enough to reject
this oft-repeated story of Trotsky's as a lie.

---

[3] This statement is also to be found three times in Chapter 12 of the English language edition of Trotsky's biography of Stalin. But this book was not completed at
Trotsky's death. It was completed by Charles Malamuth, who was later criticized
for adding materials of his own. (My thanks to David Walters for this information.) It is not in the Russian version edited by Iurii Fel'shtinsky from, he says, the
copy in the TA. But of course it would not be, for that volume only goes up to the
year 1917.

There is a yet more essential point: After his initial version of the story in October 1927, in which he dates Lenin's statement to 1921, Trotsky usually ties it to the discussion around the choice of Stalin as General Secretary of the Party, which took place at the XI Party Congress in March-April 1922.

This is how we know Trotsky was lying. First, because initially even Trotsky did not connect the story with Stalin's appointment. Second, because, by all accounts, it was Lenin himself who proposed Stalin as General Secretary.

Iurii Fel'shtinsky is a prominent and devoted Russian Trotskyist scholar who, predictably, hates Stalin. Fel'shtinsky writes:

> Отметим, что до начала болезни Ленина никаких политических разногласий между Лениным и Сталиным не было. (Vozhdy 250)

Translated:

> We note that before the onset of Lenin's illness there were no political disagreements between Lenin and Stalin.

The XI Party Congress took place immediately *before* Lenin became ill.

Fel'shtinsky does not cite any other source for the "peppery dishes" statement. In fact he does not endorse it himself but merely quotes Trotsky's text (p. 274). He then goes on to quote (p. 333, note 5) Lenin's ringing endorsement of Stalin at this 11th Party Congress from the Russian edition of Lenin's *Complete Collected Works*:

> Вот Преображенский здесь легко бросал, что Сталин в двух комиссариатах А кто не грешен из нас. Кто не брал несколько обязанностей сразу. Да и как можно делать иначе. Что мы можем сейчас сделать, чтобы было обеспечено существующее положение в Наркомнаце, чтобы разбираться со всеми туркестанскими, кавказскими и прочими вопросами. Ведь это все

политические вопросы. А разрешать эти вопросы
необходимо, это - вопросы, которые сотни лет занимали
европейские государства, которые в ничтожной доле
разрешены в демократических республиках. Мы их
разрешаем, и нам нужно, чтобы у нас был человек, к
которому любой из представителей наций мог бы пойти и
подробно рассказать, в чем дело. Где его разыскать. Я
думаю, и Преображенский не мог бы назвать другой
кандидатуры, кроме товарища Сталина. [4]

Translated:

> Here is Preobrazhensky casually tossing out the remark
> that Stalin is head of two commissariats. But who among
> us is not guilty of the same thing? Who has not taken
> several responsibilities at the same time? Moreover, how
> could it be otherwise? What can we do now to guarantee
> the current situation in the Commissariat of Nationali-
> ties, to deal with all the Turkestan, Caucasus, and other
> questions? For these are all political problems. And it is
> essential to resolve these problems. These are problems
> that have occupied European powers for centuries and
> which are scarcely resolved in the democratic republics.
> We are resolving them and we need a man whom any of
> the national representatives can approach and explain in
> detail what is the matter. Where can we find him? I think
> that even Preobrazhensky could not name another can-
> didate besides comrade Stalin.

Abdurakhman Avtorkhanov, a ferociously anti-Stalin writer, stated
that Stalin was elected General Secretary on April 3, 1922, "at
Lenin's proposal."

---

[4] Lenin, *Polnoe Sobranie Sochinenii* 45, p. 122. At http://nglib-
free.ru/book_view.jsp?idn=001579&page=122&format=html Also in the
transcript of the 11ᵗʰ Party Congress: *XI съезд РКП (б). 27 марта —2 апреля
1922 г.* — М.: Партиздат, 1936, p. 150 (March 27). This is the first edition of the
transcript of this Party Congress (Worldcat Accession Number 83723613).

Еще при первом послесталинском "коллективном руководстве" вышел Энциклопедический словарь, где в биографии Сталина прямо и недвусмысленно написано следующее: "После XI съезда партии, 3 апреля 1922 пленум Центрального Комитета партии по предложению В. И. Ленина избрал И. В. Сталина генеральным секретарем ЦК партии. На этом посту И. В. Сталин работал д о о к т я б р я 1 9 5 2, а затем до конца своей жизни являлся с е к р е т а р е м Ц К" (разрядка моя. - А. А.) (Энциклопедический словарь в 3 томах. М. 1955, т. III, стр. 310).[5]

Translated:

During the first post-Stalin period of "collective leadership" the *Encyclopedic dictionary* was published, where in the biography of Stalin we find written, directly and unequivocally, the following: "After the XI Congress of the Party, on April 3, 1922, the Plenum of the Central Committee of the Party, according to the proposal of V.I. Lenin, elected J.V. Stalin as General Secretary of the CC of the Party. J.V. Stalin worked at this post until October 1952, and then until his death was Secretary of the CC" (emphasis mine – A.A.). – [*Encyclopedic dictionary in 3 volumes.* Moscow, 1955, vol. 3, p. 310].

Molotov agrees and even says that Lenin worked hard to overcome objections to this proposal.

— Неожиданно для себя в 1921 году я стал Секретарем ЦК. Из трех секретарей был секретариат: Молотов, Ярославский, Михайлов, как было опубликовано, Молотов — Ответственный секретарь. Не было тогда еще первого, генерального, был ответственный. Приемные дни были опубликованы. Я встретился с Лениным. Мы с ним побеседовали по ряду вопросов, потом гуляли по Кремлю.

---

[5] А. Авторханов *Загадки смерти Сталина.* Барнаул. Алтайское книжное издательство, 1993. At - http://mario21.narod.ru/docs/stalin/7.htm Also in *Novyi Mir* 1991, p. 205.

Он говорит: «Только я вам советую: вы должны как Секретарь ЦК заниматься политической работой, всю техническую работу — на замов и помощников. Вот был у нас до сих пор Секретарем ЦК Крестинский, так он был управделами, а не Секретарь ЦК! Всякой ерундой занимался, а не политикой!»

Это — после X съезда партии. А на XI съезде появился так называемый «список десятки» — фамилии предполагаемых членов ЦК, сторонников Ленина. И против фамилии Сталина рукой Ленина было написано: «Генеральный секретарь». Ленин организовал фракционное собрание «десятки». Где-то возле Свердловского зала Кремля комнату нашел, уговорились: фракционное собрание, троцкистов — нельзя, рабочую оппозицию — нельзя, демократический централизм тоже не приглашать, только одни крепкие сторонники «десятки», то есть ленинцы. Собрал, по-моему, человек двадцать от наиболее крупных организаций перед голосованием. Сталин даже упрекнул Ленина, дескать, у нас секретное или полусекретное совещание во время съезда, как-то фракционно получается, а Ленин говорит: «Товарищ Сталин, вы-то старый, опытный фракционер! Не сомневайтесь, нам сейчас нельзя иначе. Я хочу, чтобы все были хорошо подготовлены к голосованию, надо предупредить товарищей, чтобы твердо голосовали за этот список без поправок! Список «десятки» надо провести целиком. Есть большая опасность, что станут голосовать по лицам, добавлять: вот этот хороший литератор, его надо, этот хороший оратор — и разжижат список, опять у нас не будет большинства. А как тогда руководить!»

А ведь на X съезде Ленин запретил фракции.

И голосовали с этим примечанием в скобках. **Сталин стал Генеральным. Ленину это больших трудов стоило.** Но он, конечно, вопрос достаточно глубоко продумал и дал понять, на кого равняться. Ленин, видимо, посчитал, что я недостаточный политик, но в секретарях и в Политбюро меня оставил, а Сталина сделал Генеральным. Он, конечно, готовился, чувствуя болезнь свою. Видел ли он в Сталине своего преемника? Думаю, что и это могло учитываться. А для чего нужен был Генеральный секретарь? Никогда не было. Но постепенно авторитет Сталина поднялся и вырос в гораздо большее, чем предполагал Ленин или чем он даже считал желательным. Но предвидеть все, конечно, было невозможно, а в условиях острой борьбы вокруг Сталина все более сколачивалась активная группа — Дзержинский, Куйбышев, Фрунзе и другие, очень разные люди.[6]

Translated:

Unexpectedly, in 1921, I became a Secretary of the Central Committee. The Secretariat was comprised of three secretaries: Molotov, Yaroslavsky, and Mikhailov. As has been published, Molotov was executive secretary. There was not at that time a first or General Secretary but an executive secretary. Reception days were made public. I met with Lenin. We discussed a number of questions and then walked around the Kremlin. He said: "But I advise you: as Secretary of the CC you must take care of the political work. Leave, all the technical work to your second-in-command and assistants. Here we had until now Krestinsky as Secretary of the Central Committee but he was a business manager, not Secretary of the CC! He occupied himself with every trivial matter but not with politics!"

This was after the X Congress of the Party. And at the XI Congress appeared the so-called "list of ten" - the names of proposed members of the Central Committee, Lenin's supporters. And beside Stalin's name in Lenin's hand was written: "General Secretary." Lenin organized a factional meeting of the "ten." Somewhere near Sverdlovsk

---

[6] Felix Chuev, *Molotov. Poluderzhavniy Vlastelin*, pp. 239-241. This is an expanded version of the book published in English as *Molotov Remembers*.

Hall of the Kremlin I found a room. They were persuaded: this is a factional meeting, Trotskyists, workers'
opposition, the Democratic Centralists – don't invite
them, only the firm supporters of the "ten," that is, the
Leninists. I gathered, I think, about twenty people from
among the strongest organizations before the vote. Stalin even reproached Lenin, saying that we are having a
secret or semi-secret meeting during the convention,
something factional is taking place, and Lenin said:
"Comrade Stalin, you are an old, experienced factionalist!
Have no doubt, we can't do otherwise now. I want eve-
ryone to be well prepared for the vote, it is necessary to
warn the comrades to vote for this list without amend-
ment! We need to carry through with the list of 'ten' as a
whole. There is a great danger that if people vote for individuals they will say: Here is a good writer, we need
him; this is a good speaker – they will tear up this sheet
and once again we will not have the majority. And then,
how can we lead!"

But at the X Congress, Lenin had banned factions.

And they voted with this note in brackets. **Stalin became General Secretary. This cost Lenin a lot of
work.** But he, of course, had thought through the question deeply enough and made it clear who to rely on.
Lenin apparently decided that I was not enough of a
politician, but he left me as a Secretary and in the Politburo and made Stalin General Secretary. He, of course,
was preparing himself, feeling his sickness. Did he see
Stalin as his successor? I think you can count on that. But
what was the need for a General Secretary? There had
never been one. But gradually Stalin's authority rose and
grew into something much larger than Lenin had anticipated or even though desirable. But of course it was impossible to foresee everything, and under conditions of
sharp struggle an active group began to form itself

around Stalin -- Dzerzhinsky, Kuibyshev, Frunze and others, very different people.

Robert Service cites Molotov here, and does not question what he says. For Service, Lenin either "chose Stalin" or "supported a proposal" by someone else.

> **He [Lenin] was eager to have Stalin back at his side.** Having recruited him to the Leninist cause in the trade union dispute, Lenin supported a proposal to make him General Secretary of the Russian Communist Party.
>
> Conventionally it has been supposed that Stalin was put in office because he was an experienced bureaucrat with an unusual capacity for not being bored by administrative work. The facts do not bear this out.... The reason why Lenin chose Stalin was less administrative than political. He wanted one of his allies in a post crucial to the maintenance of his policies. (Stalin 189-190)

Other sources agree that at the XI Party Congress Lenin nominated Stalin to the post of General Secretary.

Stalin was formally appointed on April 3, 1922, at the first meeting of the new Central Committee after the Congress. In fact, I cannot find any source that disagrees – except, implicitly, Trotsky, and Trotskyist writers who just echo what Trotsky later wrote.

Trotsky contradicted himself about when Lenin supposedly made the remark, under what circumstances, and who heard him make it. Therefore the "peppery dishes" story is a lie.

But Trotsky told it over and over again, many times over a number of years. Eventually he even called it Lenin's "famous remark." This is a propaganda technique: claim the remark is so "famous" that "everybody knows it" and so no evidence for it is necessary.

It's easy to see why Trotsky liked this story and wanted others to believe it. It made him appear as though he had been close to Lenin, part of the "small circle," one of Lenin's "most intimate comrades." It made Stalin look like someone whom Lenin opposed from a date much earlier than 1923, when Lenin was very ill.

But how could Trotsky think that he could get away with repeating this lie over and over again? For one thing, it would not have been easy to refute it in the 1930s. The proceedings of the XI Congress were not published until 1936. Very few people would have bothered to check them. The rest of the sources I cite here were not to be published for many years.

We should also consider to whom Trotsky was addressing this and the other lies I document in this work. This was, in the main, his supporters, the Trotskyists. Who else was reading Trotsky's materials?[7]

Trotsky's followers *believed* Trotsky. Virtually no one else did. And Trotsky wanted his own followers to believe that he, not Stalin, had been Lenin's closest associate. Trotsky's essays were published primarily in Russian in his *Biulleten' Oppozitsii*. Many were translated and distributed in pamphlets and in newspapers but always by Trotsky's own supporters.

This specific lie of Trotsky's is relatively easy to expose today. But I can't find that it has been exposed before. One might think that members of the Trotskyist movement might have done so. After all, few other people in the world are really interested in Trotsky, really motivated to study his works carefully and use them in judging Soviet history.

I noted above that Iurii Fel'shtinsky noticed this incongruity between Trotsky's "peppery dishes" tale and the reality that Lenin had proposed Stalin as General Secretary. But even Fel'shtinsky, surely among the most capable Trotskyist historians today, did not

---

[7] Trotsky also wrote articles for the capitalist press. Naturally, whatever lies he told in his own publications had to be repeated there too. But readers of the capitalist press were not his primary audience.

come out and state: "Trotsky must have been lying; he must have fabricated this story," etc.

Whatever the difficulty of uncovering this specific lie of Trotsky's, it is much harder to discover those of Trotsky's lies that I discuss and utilize as evidence in this book. I was only able to find them because I was looking for them. I was guided by the hypothesis that Trotsky often lied. This hypothesis suggested itself after studying the research of Pierre Broué, Arch Getty, and Sven-Eric Holmström. They had revealed the fact that Trotsky lied about important matters.

At length it occurred to me to wonder: "If Trotsky lied about these things, maybe he also lied about other important things as well." Only then did I begin to look for other lies by Trotsky. And, sure enough, I discovered some.

The Structure of This Book

Trotsky's "peppery dishes" lie is, in terms of its practical impact, not very important. I include it here because this lie is indicative of Trotsky's overall character and reliability. As we will see in other contexts many times, Trotsky lied a lot!

Trotsky was not afraid to lie even when it was not important, at that moment, to tell that particular lie. After all, in telling this "cook ... peppery dishes" lie Trotsky took some chance that his lie would be discovered.

But what did he stand to gain by telling it that he would not have gained if he had not told it? Nothing, as far I can determine. True, it suggests that a clear-headed Lenin opposed Stalin, something Trotsky wished others to believe. But if he had never told this particular lie no one would have missed it, because no one would have expected it in the first place. Probably no one became a Trotskyist, or gave money to the Trotskyist movement, just because of this story. The most one can say for this fable is that it is consistent with Trotsky's overall project of presenting himself as Lenin's closest confidant, his best student, and therefore his rightful heir.

Perhaps this is the reason that Trotsky was willing to lie repeatedly even when there was little gain to be had and despite the fact that there was always a risk of being exposed as a liar. And that *was* a possibility. Anyone who found that speech of Trotsky's in the November 2, 1927, issue of *Pravda* and compared the "cook ... peppery dishes" version there with the way Trotsky told it repeatedly during the 1930s could easily see that Trotsky had changed his story.

This gives us a very interesting insight into the mind of Trotsky. It reflects a kind of bravado or arrogance: "I can make stuff up, and people will believe it." How much more, therefore, should we expect Trotsky to be willing to lie when there *was* something important at stake, something substantial to be gained by lying and/or to be lost by not lying? Under such circumstances we should expect Trotsky to lie readily, whenever he thought it expedient to do so. And that is exactly what I have found.

In the present book I examine some interesting and bold lies by Trotsky that I have discovered, and consider the implications of those lies. I will argue that, together with other evidence, Trotsky's lies reveal much about his clandestine conspiratorial activities. Moreover, what they reveal is consistent both with Moscow Trials testimony – testimony whose validity we can now accept, having tested and proven it in Part One of *Trotsky's 'Amalgams'* and in *The Moscow Trials as Evidence* – and with other primary source evidence.

Trotsky's lies – those discovered first by others like Broué, Getty, and Holmström, and some that I have discovered – are central to understanding Trotsky himself, the Opposition conspiracies, the Moscow Trials, the Tukhachevsky Affair, or Military Purges – in short, all the high politics of the Soviet Union during the 1930s. The book as a whole can be read as a commentary on some very interesting falsehoods that Trotsky chose to propagate, and which he was, on the whole, successful at getting others to believe. Indeed, they are still widely believed today.

The facts uncovered and discussed in this book should be of great interest to those who wish to learn the truth about the high politics of the Soviet Union during the 1930s, and also those who have a genuine interest in the prominent political actors of that period, including Trotsky himself.

* * * * *

All boldface emphases are by me unless otherwise noted.

I would like to express my special thanks to Bill Sacks, whose advice and criticism has been more helpful than I can truly say; to Mike Bessler, my tireless publisher, editor, and friend; and to Dr. Susana M. Sotillo, incisive critic, great scholar, and supportive *compañera*.

Chapter 2. Trotsky on the Kirov
Assassination

On December 1, 1934 Sergei M. Kirov, First Secretary of the Bolshevik party in Leningrad, Politburo member, and close associate
of Joseph Stalin, was murdered outside his office by Leonid Nikolaev, an unemployed party member. Nikolaev then tried to commit
suicide but failed and was captured. Within a few days he had
named as his accomplices a number of members of an underground group of Party members loyal to Grigory Zinoviev, whom
Kirov had replaced as Leningrad party chief.

Study of the discoveries made during the past several decades in
the Harvard Trotsky Archive and of documents from former Soviet
archives published since the end of the USSR permits us to read
Trotsky's writings on the Kirov assassination in a new light. Trotsky's article purports to be an attempt to understand the Kirov
assassination by scrutinizing the Soviet government's reporting
about it.

But now we can see that it is not this at all. Rather, Trotsky's article is a cover-up, an attempt to use lies and misdirection to keep
hidden Trotsky's and his followers' involvement in a bloc with the
clandestine Zinovievist group that did carry out Kirov's murder.

The *Biulleten' Oppozitsii* – in English, the Bulletin of the [Russian]
Opposition (henceforth B.O.) – was Leon Trotsky's periodical journal during the years between his expulsion from the Soviet Union
1929 and his assassination in August 1940. Written and published
in Russian, it has never been translated in its entirety. However,
many of Trotsky's individual articles, published first in the B.O.,
have been translated and published separately. In the case of B.O.
#41 of January 1935, a single article of Trotsky's occupied an en-
tire issue. I have verified that the English version, titled "The Stalinist Bureaucracy and the Assassination of Kirov," is a faithful

translation of the entire issue #41 of the B.O. and will use the English translation here.[1]

"Amalgam"

I need to say something about Trotsky's frequent use of the word "amalgam." In Russian *amal'gama* can be used to mean any kind of mixture or combination. Trotsky uses it very frequently in Russian to mean something like "false account of events." Following Trotsky's practice his English translators employ the word "amalgam." Trotsky uses the word "amalgam" two dozen times in this one article alone. He defines it in the following way:

> It was clear, however, that this information relating to the "Zinoviev group" was not issued by accident; it could imply nothing else but the preparation of a jural "amalgam," that is to say, a consciously false attempt to implicate in the assassination of Kirov **individuals and groups who did not and could not have anything in common with the terrorist act.**

One noteworthy result of my research is the discovery that it was not Stalin but rather Trotsky himself who composed "amalgams" the "consciously false" accounts of events surrounding the Kirov murder.

Trotsky's own "amalgams" – one of which was the charge that it was Stalin who was composing "amalgams" – served Trotsky's aims in two ways. First, they were an attempt to discredit accusations made by the Soviet prosecution against the various oppositionists. All of these men had been followers of Trotsky's, had worked closely with Trotsky, or were followers of one or more of

---

[1] "Leon Trotsky: On the Kirov Assassination (December 1934)." At http://www.marxists.org/archive/trotsky/1934/12/kirov.htm Unless otherwise identified, all quotations attributed to Trotsky here are to this two-part article. The Russian original of *Biulleten' Oppozitsii* is at http://www.mit.edu/people/fjk/BO/BO-41.html and at http://www.1917.com/Marxism/Trotsky/BO/BO_No_41/Main.html

the oppositionists who, like Zinoviev, had worked closely with Trotsky.

Second, by accusing Stalin of composing "amalgams," i.e. of lying, Trotsky deflected attention away from his own falsehoods. Since many of these lies of Trotsky's could have easily been discovered if anyone had checked, perhaps the only effective "smokescreen" or cover-up at Trotsky's disposal was to call Stalin the liar first.

Trotsky listed the fifteen Moscow-based Zinovievists whose arrests had been announced in *Pravda*. Two of those arrested were Grigory Zinoviev and Lev Kamenev, who we know were part of the bloc of Trotskyists and Zinovievists formed with Trotsky's permission in 1932. A third was Safarov, a Zinoviev follower whom Leon Sedov, Trotsky's son and his main political aide, had identified in 1932 as one who would shortly join the bloc.[2] I have reproduced the texts of Sedov's and Trotsky's letters about the bloc at the end of the present volume.

We have independent evidence from Soviet archives that Safarov was recruiting others to this same bloc in August 1932. According to this testimony Safarov was telling others that the bloc had regular contact with Trotsky,[3] a fact confirmed by materials in the Harvard Trotsky Archive.

В августе 1932 г. я был у него в Москве на улице Грановского, 5 в Доме советов. САФАРОВ, убедившись в неизменности моих антисоветских убеждений, сообщил

---

[2] Letters by Trotsky and his son Leon Sedov discussing the formation of the bloc in 1932 and its composition were discovered in 1980 in the Harvard Trotsky Archive by Pierre Broué, at the time the most prominent Trotskyist historian in the world. Broué reported these findings, including a letter naming Zinoviev, Kamenev, Safarov and others in Pierre Broué, "Trotsky et le bloc des oppositions de 1932." CahLT 5 (1980) 5-37. The discovery of the bloc is discussed and the relevant part of Sedov's letter quoted in English translation in Furr Kirov 131-133.

[3] Interrogation of S. Kh. Khodzhanov, July 31, 1937. In Lubianka. 1937-1938 Document No. 155 p. 290.

мне, что зиновьевцы имеют свой конспиративный центр и в блоке с троцкистами продолжают борьбу против ЦК ВКП(б). Видя, что в лице САФАРОВА я могу найти возможного союзника нашей антисоветской организации, я в свою очередь рассказал ему, что вхожу в нелегальную националистическую антисоветскую организацию, борющуюся против ВКП(б) и советской власти. САФАРОВ выдвинул передо мной вопрос о блоке троцкистско-зиновьевского центра с нашей организацией для совместной борьбы против ВКП(б). Он также информировал меня, что у них имеется регулярная связь с ТРОЦКИМ, и они считают необходимым действовать в союзе с агрессивными странами.

Translated:

In August 1932 I was with him in Moscow at 5 Granovsky Street, in the Palace of Soviets. SAFAROV, convinced that my anti-Soviet convictions had not changed, informed me that the Zinovievists had their conspiratorial center and in a bloc with the Trotskyists were continuing the struggle against the CC of the VKP(b). Seeing that in SAFAROV I could find a possible ally for our anti-Soviet organization, I told him in turn that I had joined an illegal nationalist anti-Soviet organization that was struggling against the VKP(b) and against Soviet authority. SAFAROV posed the question of a bloc between the Trotskyist-Zinovievist center and our organization for mutual struggle against the VKP(b). He also informed me that they had regular contact with TROTSKY, and that they considered it essential to act in concert with aggressor countries.

The fact that we know from the Trotsky Archive that the bloc existed and included both Trotskyists and Zinovievists, as Khodzhanov testifies here, is further evidence that the NKVD was *not* falsifying interrogation-confessions. In Part One of *Trotsky's 'Amalgams'* and in *The Moscow Trials as Evidence* I set forth a great deal of evidence that the Moscow Trials testimony is genuine – that is, it represents what the defendants chose to say.

Trotsky did his best to distance himself from Zinoviev and Kamenev by attacking them:

> There is not the slightest reason or motive for us to defend the policies or personal reputations of Zinoviev, Kamenev and their friends. They were at the head of that faction which inaugurated the struggle against Marxist internationalism under the name of "Trotskyism"; they were subsequently driven against the bureaucratic wall raised with their own efforts and under their own leadership; having taken fright at their own handiwork, they joined the Left Opposition for a brief period and revealed the frauds and falsehoods utilized in the struggle against "Trotskyism"; frightened by the difficulties of the struggle against the usurping bureaucracy, they capitulated; reinstated to the party, they substituted for principled opposition, sniping, secret machinations; they were again expelled – they capitulated for the second time.
>
> They disavowed the banner of Marxism and camouflaged themselves, hoping to gain a place in the party which had been corrupted and strangled by the apparatus. Having generally lost esteem and confidence, and even the possibility of waging a struggle, they found themselves, in the end, cruelly punished. It is not our task to defend them!

These paragraphs are a lie. We know now that Trotsky and his Soviet-based followers really were in a bloc with Zinoviev, Kamenev, Safarov, and others. That means that this verbal assault by Trotsky on Zinoviev, Kamenev "and their friends" was a cover-up intended to mask Trotsky's real relations with these men through the bloc. It was a part of Trotsky's "amalgam." Likewise, Trotsky often wrote sharp attacks on Karl Radek claiming that, on principle, he had not been in any contact, direct or indirect, with Radek, when in fact we know that he had indeed written Radek at exactly the time

Radek disclosed during his testimony at the January 1937 Moscow Trial.[4]

Documents from Trotsky's own archive now permit us to see that in the cases of Zinoviev, Kamenev, and Radek Trotsky's attacks were a cover for conspiratorial ties. *Therefore we cannot take any of Trotsky's attacks on any opposition figures at face value.*

Trotsky argued that Zinoviev and Kamenev "could not" have been involved in Kirov's assassination on two grounds. First, because these "old Bolsheviks, the most intimate collaborators of Lenin, those who shared power with Stalin, members of the 'Old Guard,'" could not possibly "have posed for their task the *restoration of capitalism.*" Second, because Bolshevism and Marxism-Leninism firmly prohibit "individual terror" (assassination).[5]

"Terror"

Trotsky insisted that the Zinovievists could not be involved in the assassination of Kirov because terrorism is incompatible with Marxism.

> The negative attitude of Marxism towards the tactic of individual terror is known to every worker able to read and write. A great deal has been written on this question.

Therefore, Trotsky asserted, Zinoviev and Kamenev could not have been involved in Kirov's murder.

---

[4] Evidence of this letter was discovered in the Harvard Trotsky Archive by American historian J. Arch Getty. See Getty TIE 24-35. For the evidence that this letter was the one Radek mentioned in his testimony at the January 1937 Moscow Trial (sometimes called the "Radek-Piatakov Trial" or "Second Moscow Trial") see Furr, Kirov, 321. We discuss this matter in detail in another chapter of the present book.

[5] A careful reading of all the Soviet materials related to the Kirov murder and published during December 1934 reveals that Zinoviev and Kamenev were not, in fact, accused of plotting "the restoration of capitalism." We explore this apparently unaccountable remark of Trotsky's in a later chapter.

Zinoviev and Kamenev were lacking in character, but no one considered them fools or ignorant buffoons. The other thirteen above named Bolsheviks lived through the experiences of the Bolshevik party for 25-30 and more years. They could not suddenly turn to a belief in the utility of individual terror for changing the social régime ...

Nor, says Trotsky, could he himself be suspected of stooping to terror. Quoting from an article of his own published in 1911 he continued:

To this article which counterposed to terrorist adventurism the method of preparing the proletariat for the socialist revolution, I can add nothing today, twenty-three years later.

Trotsky theorized that terrorists were guilty of the same kind of cult-of-great-man thinking as he discerned in the Soviet party.

Individual terrorism is in its very essence bureaucratism turned inside out. For Marxists this law was not discovered yesterday. Bureaucratism has no confidence in the masses, and endeavors to substitute itself for the masses. Terrorism works in the same manner; it seeks to make the masses happy without asking their participation. The Stalinist bureaucracy has created a vile leader-cult, attributing to leaders divine qualities. "Hero" worship is also the religion of terrorism, only with a minus sign.

Then he uses language similar to that used by his son Leon Sedov when talking to Mark Zborowski in January 1937.

Trotsky, December – January 1934-1935: "The Nikolaievs imagine that all that is necessary is to remove a few leaders by means of a revolver in order for history to take another course."

> *Sedov, January 1937*: "While he was reading newspapers 'Sonny'[6] said that since the whole regime in the USSR is held up by Stalin, it would be enough to kill Stalin for it all to fall apart."

Trotsky and Terror

Mark Zborowski was an NKVD agent who managed to gain Sedov's confidence. Zborowski wrote reports to his handlers while acting as one of Sedov's closest collaborators. In a report dated February 8, 1937, Zborowski wrote that on January 22, 1937, the eve of the Piatakov-Radek trial, Sedov suddenly began speaking to him of "terror":

> February 8, 1937
>
> On January 22 L. Sedov in our conversation at his apartment about the question of the second Moscow trial and the role in it of some of the accused (Radek, Piatakov and others) stated: "Now there is no reason to hesitate. Stalin must be killed."
>
> For me this statement was so unexpected that I did not manage to react to it in any way. L. Sedov immediately redirected the conversation onto other questions.
>
> On January 23 L. Sedov, in my presence and also that of L. Estrina, uttered a sentence with the same content as that of the 22nd. In answer to this statement of his L. Estrina said: "Keep your mouth shut." They did not return to this question again.[7]

---

6 "Sonny" (Russian synok) was the NKVD code name for Sedov. Pierre Broué rendered synok in French as "le fiston."

7 Zborowski archive, F.31660 d. 9067 Papka No. 28. In Volkogonov Archive, Library of Congress. Online at
http://msuweb.montclair.edu/~furrg/research/zbor_sedov_stalin0238.pdf
Some of these same documents are confirmed by John Costello and Oleg Tsarev, *Deadly Illusions* (New York: Crown, 1993) , 283; 469 n.44. Tsarev, a former KGB

Trotsky claimed that terrorism was in violation of Marxism:

> But if Marxists categorically condemned individual ter-
> rorism, obviously for political and not mystical reasons,
> even when the shots were directed against the agents of
> the Czarist government and of capitalist exploitation,
> they will even more relentlessly condemn and reject the
> criminal adventurism of terrorist acts directed against
> the bureaucratic representatives of the first workers'
> state in history.

But in 1937 Sedov justified terrorism to Zborowski in language
similar to what I.I. Reingol'd, a codefendant in the 1936 Moscow
Trial, attributed to Zinoviev and Kamenev, and that another codefendant, K.B. Berman-Iuriin attributed directly to Trotsky.

Reingol'd:

> VYSHINSKY: How did Zinoviev and Kamenev reconcile
> terroristic activities with Marxism?

> REINGOLD: In 1932, Zinoviev, at Kamenev's apartment,
> in the presence of a number of members of the united
> Trotskyist-Zinovievite centre argued in favor of resort-
> ing to terror as follows: although terror is incompatible
> with Marxism, at the present moment these considera-
> tions must be abandoned. There are no other methods
> available of fighting the leaders of the Party and the
> Government at the present time. Stalin combines in him-
> self all the strength and firmness of the present Party

---

man, had privileged access to KGB files for a time in the early 1990s. The same
texts are quoted in Tsarev & Kostello, *Rokovye Illiuzii*, 322-3, and n. 44 p.531
(Russian original). These and other texts of Zborowski's reports are in facsimile
in the Volkogonov Archive, LOC. This archive also contains facsimiles of the
reports published by Costello and Tsarev, thus verifying that they are the same
ones.

leadership. Therefore Stalin must be put out of the way in the first place. (1936 Trial 55)

Berman-Iuriin:

> In the evening we continued our conversation. I asked him how individual terrorism could be reconciled with Marxism. To this Trotsky replied: problems cannot be treated in a dogmatic way. He said that a situation had arisen in the Soviet Union which Marx could not have foreseen. (1936 Trial 95)

Zborowski:

> С 1936 г. «сынок» не вел со мной разговоров о терроре. Лишь недели две-три тому назад, после собрания группы «сынок» снова заговорил на эту тему. В первый раз он только старался «теоретически» доказать, что терроризм не противоречит марксизму. «Марксизм» -- по словам сынка – «отрицает терроризм постолько, поscolько условия классовой борьбы не благоприпятствует терроризму, но бывают такие положения, в которых терроризм необходим.» В следующий раз «сынок» заговорил о терроризме, когда я пришел к нему на квартиру работать. Во время читки газет «Сынок» сказал, что так как весь режим в СССР держится на Сталине, то достаточно убить Сталина, чтобы все развалилась. Эту мысль он высказывал и раньше, но до последнего раза он никогда ее так четко не формулировал. В этот последний раз он неоднократно возвращался к этому, и особенно тщательно подчеркивал необходимость убийства тов. Сталина.

Translated:

> Since 1936 "Sonny" had not talked with me about terror. Only about two or three weeks ago, after a meeting of the group, "Sonny" again began to speak on this subject. At first he only tried to "theoretically" prove that terrorism does not contradict Marxism. "Marxism" – in Sonny's words – "rejects terrorism only insofar as the conditions

of the class struggle are not suitable for terrorism, but there are situations in which terrorism is essential."

The next time "Sonny" began to speak about terrorism when I arrived at his apartment to work. While reading newspapers "Sonny" said that since the whole regime of the USSR is held up by Stalin, it would be enough to kill Stalin for everything to fall apart. He had stated this thought earlier too, but until this time he had never formulated it this sharply. This last time he repeatedly returned to it, and underscored with special care the necessity to kill com. Stalin.

Sedov tried to recruit Zborowski as a terrorist to kill Stalin:

> В связи с этим разговором «сынок» спросил меня боюсь ли я смерти вообще и способен ли я был совершить террористичесий акт.

Translated:

> In connection with this talk "Sonny" asked me whether I feared death in general, and whether I would be capable of committing a terrorist act.

When Zborowski temporized without giving a definite answer Sedov outlined his own conception of what a terrorist must be like:

> На мой ответ что все это зависит от необходимости и целесообразности, сынок сказал, что я не совсем верно понимаю, что такое «настоящий» террорист и начал мне объяснять какими должны быть люди подходящие для исполнения терактов.
>
> Переходя к тактике террора он остановился на кадрах, считая, что это основное. Террорист – по словам сынка – должен всегда быть готовым к смерти, смерть должна быть для террориста ежедневной реальностью, причем эту тезу он иллюстрировал примером психологии народовольцев. Причем при этом он бросил реплику, что

я – по его мнению – человек слишком мягкий для такого
рода дел.

Translated:

> To my answer that everything would depend on the ne-
> cessity and the expediency, Sonny said that I did not un-
> derstand accurately at all what a "real" terrorist was and
> began to explain to me just what persons who were suit-
> able for carrying out terrorist acts must be like.

> Speaking of the tactic of terror he paused on the subject
> of cadres, saying that this was basic. A terrorist – in
> Sonny's words – must always be prepared for death;
> death must be for the terrorist a daily reality. Here he il-
> lustrated this thesis with the example of the psychology
> of the Narodovol'tsy.[8] At this point he tossed out the re-
> mark that I, in his opinion, was too soft a person for this
> kind of affair.

According to Mark Zborowski, Sedov told him on January 22, the
day *before* the Second Moscow Trial began, that Stalin should be
killed:

> 22 января Л. Седов во время нашей беседы, у него на
> квартире, по вопросу о 2-м московском процессе и роли в
> нем отдельных подсудимых (Радека, Пятакова и др.)
> заявил: "Теперь колебаться нечего. Сталина нужно убить."

Translated:

> On January 22 L. Sedov, during our conversation in his
> apartment about the question of the Second Moscow
> Trial and the roles in it of certain defendants (Radek,
> Piatakov, and others) declared: "Now there is no reason
> to hesitate. Stalin must be killed." (Emphasis in original)

---

[8] Members of the terrorist "Narodnaia Vol'ya" or "People's Will," who carried out
numerous assassinations of Tsarist officials, including that of Tsar Alexander II in
1881.

On October 28, 1936, a little fewer than three months earlier, Sedov had signed the introduction to the *Livre rouge sur le procès de Moscou* (*The Red Book on the Moscow Trial*). The *Livre rouge* repeats Trotsky's insistent claim that Marxists generally, and Trotsky himself specifically, completely eschew "terror" – individual assassination.[9] The *Bulletin of the Opposition*, Trotsky's Russian-language periodical, ##52-53 and also dated October, 1936, says exactly the same thing.

The Second Moscow Trial began on January 23, 1937. Zborowski reported:

> 23 января Л. Седов, в присутствии моем а также Л. Эстриной, бросил фразу такого же содержания как и 22-го. В ответ на это его заявление, Л. Эстрина сказала «Держи язык за зубами». Больше к этому вопросу не возвращались.

Translated:

> On January 23 L. Sedov in my presence and that of L. Estrina[10] uttered a sentence with the same content as that of the 22nd. In answer to this statement of his L. Estrina said: "Keep your mouth shut." They did not return to this question again.

It is legitimate to assume that Sedov's views on terror were also those of his father. After all, Sedov was Trotsky's main political representative. He had no political positions of his own.

---

[9] *Livre rouge* pp. 68-71, "Marxisme et terreur individuelle." The *Livre rouge* and B.O. ##52-53 are the same work. This work was translated into English as *The Red Book on the Moscow Trials*. It is online at
http://www.marxists.org/history/etol/writers/sedov/works/red/
[10] Lola or Lilia Estrina was a supporter of Trotsky's movement and secretary to Sedov.

We know from the memoir of Jules Humbert-Droz that by 1928 at the latest Bukharin was advocating the murder of Stalin.[11] The Rightist group led by Bukharin was again discussing the need to kill Stalin in 1932, the same year they united with the Trotskyists, Zinovievists, and others in the bloc.[12] If Trotsky had really opposed terror in principle, as he repeatedly proclaimed, he would not have joined a bloc with those who championed it.

Both Pierre Broué and Arch Getty have pointed out that Trotsky lied when he believed it was expedient to do so. For example, Trotsky denied the existence of the bloc, and also denied that he had written to Radek. However, Getty discovered that Trotsky had indeed written to Radek. (Getty TIE) Sven-Eric Holmström showed that Trotsky lied repeatedly concerning the "Hotel Bristol" matter.[13] Broué discovered a number of other issues Trotsky lied about.[14]

All the evidence we now have supports the hypothesis that Trotsky advocated assassination. There is no evidence to impugn this hypothesis except for Trotsky's and Sedov's public denials. We are compelled to discount their denials since we know they both lied when they thought it to their advantage to do so in the interests of their conspiratorial work, which Zborowski's reports shine a light on.

Even Pierre Broué, in his day the most prominent Trotskyist historian and researcher in the world, accepted Zborowski's reports as genuine.

---

[11] See Part One, Chapter 8 of *Trotsky's 'Amalgams'*, Chapter 8 of *The Moscow Trials As Evidence*. See also the discussion of Jules Humbert-Droz's revelation in his 1971 memoir in Grover Furr and Vladimir L. Bobrov. "Stephen Cohen's Biography of Bukharin: A Study in the Falsehood of Khrushchev-Era 'Revelations.'" *Cultural Logic* 2010 (published January 1, 2012) 1-5.
[12] Furr and Bobrov, 64-67.
[13] Holmström, New Evidence.
[14] Broué summarizes some of them in POS.

> Le général est capable de passer des documents sous si-
> lence, mais je ne le crois pas capable de falsifier un
> document. (Broué Léon Sedov 210-211)

Translated:

> The general [Dmitry Volkogonov – GF] is capable of re-
> maining silent about documents but I do not believe that
> he is capable of falsifying a document.

In a later chapter I discuss Zborowski's remarks at greater length
and note that John Costello and Oleg Tsarev have verified that they
come from Zborowski's NKVD file, to which they gained access in
the early 1990s.

Therefore we have good evidence that Trotsky was indeed advocating "terror" despite his vehement professions that he would
never do so.

The Name of Trotsky

The first of Trotsky's two essays in issue #41 of the B.O. (also in
the translation), dated December 28, 1934, does not cite any Soviet source that mentions Trotsky's name. Nevertheless, Trotsky
stated he has deduced that he himself was the real target:

> By dealing this blow to the Zinoviev group, Stalin, as we
> said, aimed at consolidating the ranks of the bureaucracy.
> But that is only one aspect of the matter. There is another,
> and no less important, side: *Using the Zinovievist group as a
> footstool, Stalin is aiming to strike a blow at Trotskyism.* And
> cost what it may, he must strike that blow. In order to un-
> derstand the goal and the direction of this new stage of the
> struggle against "Trotskyism," it is necessary to consider –
> even though briefly – the international work of the Stalinist
> faction.

As Trotsky knew then, and as we know today, he and his followers
in the USSR were in a bloc with the Zinovievists. Zinoviev, Kame-

nev, and others had been arrested. It was obvious that the Zino-vievists had already named their own leaders.

Having done that they would have no reason not to also name those with whom they had long been in a bloc: the Trotskyists. And the Trotskyists would not ally with persons who planned "ter-ror" unless Trotsky had declared that terror was necessary. We know that the bloc was in touch with Trotsky. So Trotsky had good reason to think that his name would be mentioned by the Zino-vievists.

Trotsky claimed that he had predicted this new "amalgam:"

> When the first dispatch appeared in which Nikolaiev was said to have been a member of the Leningrad Opposition in 1926, there was no further room for doubt. The new campaign against Zinoviev and Kamenev was not long in following. **At that moment, in a conversation with a friend (I apologize for these personal details, but they are necessary for the understanding of the psy-chological undercurrents in the case), I said, "The matter will not rest long on this plane; tomorrow they will bring Trotskyism to the fore." To be able to make such a prediction, it was really not necessary to be a prophet.** The December 25 issue of the *Temps* which I received two or three days later contained in a telegraphic dispatch from Moscow the following item: "We must point out ... that as the days go by, Trotsky's name is being mentioned more and more often alongside Zinoviev's." [3] Kirov's corpse and the Zinoviev group thus become preparatory steps for a much wider and bolder scheme: to deal a blow at international Leninism.

Trotsky's name was indeed mentioned, but only because the French newspaper had misidentified as a Trotskyist Grigori Evdokimov, a Zinovievist arrested on December 9 in connection with the Kirov investigation. This was an easy error to make be-cause Evdokimov had been identified as a Trotskyist when, along with many others, he had been expelled from the Party in 1927. Trotsky would have known this.[15]

"Expose the Scheme In Advance"

Trotsky claimed that he had deduced that his name would be mentioned and publicized this in order to "expose the scheme in advance."

> There is only one way to forestall en route the amalgams that are in preparation: *Expose the scheme in advance.* The Stalinists are trying to mold the public opinion of the world police towards expulsions, extraditions, arrests and other more decisive measures. The Leninists must prepare the public opinion of the world proletariat for these possible events. In this case, as in others, it is necessary to speak out openly about what is; that is also the aim of the present article.

We know today that the NKVD's connecting Trotsky with the Zinovievists was not a "scheme" but the truth. Evidently, Trotsky hoped to make what was true appear so patently false as to be predictable in advance and so to dissipate any suspicion about his activities. It was Trotsky's story that was the real "amalgam."

"The Indictment"

In the same issue #41 of B.O. (and in the same English translation) Trotsky published an article titled "The Indictment" and dated it

---

[15] Page 2 of the December 25, 1934, issue of the Paris newspaper *Le Temps* did carry an article that contained these words – but only because of the arrest on December 10 (he was actually arrested on December 9) of Grigori Evdokimov. Evdokimov had been expelled from the Party at the XV Party Congress in 1927 as "an active member of the Trotskyist opposition." Evdokimov is listed in *XV S"ezd Vsesoiuznoi Kommunisticheskoi Partii – (b). Stenograficheskii otchet* (Moscow: Gosudarstvennoe Izdatel'stvo, 1928), p. 1247, No. 17 and page 1318 No. 18. Evdokimov was No. 31 of 121 persons who signed a letter dated December 3, 1927, agreeing to the Party's line and requesting reinstatement; see *ibid.*, p. 1334.

December 30, 1934, two days after the first. In it Trotsky claimed that he was examining the summary of the indictment of the Kirov defendants that was published in the French Communist Party's newspaper *Humanité* of December 28, 1934, along with a short introductory front-page article by future French CP leader Jacques Duclos.

This article by Trotsky contains a number of revealing remarks that we need to examine carefully. I have obtained a copy of this issue of *Humanité* so we can compare Trotsky's remarks against the text of the articles upon which he is commenting.[16]

Trotsky begins:

> Just as one could have expected, **the indictment doesn't mention the Zinoviev-Kamenev group by so much as a word**. In other words: the initial amalgam fell apart into dust.

Anyone who reads the *Humanité* article in question can see that Trotsky is lying here. The indictment mentions the Zinoviev-Kamenev group repeatedly. Here are the relevant passages from the article in *Humanité*:

> "...des participants de l'ancien **groupe antisoviétique Zinoviev**" (col. 1);

> "...par les chefs de **notre organization: Zinoviev, Kamenev** et autres..." (col. 1);

> "...pour cacher la participation du **groupe Zinoviev**" (col. 3)

---

16 Short front-page article: "L'acte d'accusation de Nikolaiev montre la complicité de Trotski dans l'assassinat de Kirov" par Jacques Duclos. Summary and discussion of the indictment: "La Révolution se défend. L'acte d'accusation contre Nikolaiev et ses complices terroristes révèle l'activité contre-révolutionnaire du groupe zinovieviste," page 3.

"... les anciens members du **groupe antisoviétique Zi-noviev...**" (col. 4);

Therefore, Trotsky's claim that "the initial amalgam fell apart into dust" is false as well. On the contrary: once more the "amalgam," or "consciously false" story, is by Trotsky.

Immediately after the words quoted above Trotsky wrote the following:

> However, concurrently it has fulfilled its task by psychologically preparing for another amalgam: in the indictment there emerges suddenly – suddenly for naive people – the name of Trotsky. Nikolaiev, the murderer of Kirov, was – according to his confession – in contact with a consul of a foreign power. During one of Nikolaiev's visits to the consulate, the consul gave him 5,000 roubles for expenses. Nikolaiev adds, "He told me that he can establish contact with Trotsky, if I give him a letter to Trotsky from the group." And that is all. Period! The indictment does not subsequently return to this episode. ... But how and why does my name suddenly appear here? **Is it, perhaps, because the terrorist group was seeking contact with Trotsky? No, even the GPU does not dare to assert this.** Perhaps Trotsky was seeking contact with the terrorist group? No, the indictment does not dare say this either. **The consul himself was the one to assume the initiative** and, while giving Nikolaiev *5,000 roubles on the eve of the terrorist act that was being prepared, he requested a letter addressed to Trotsky.*

This statement of Trotsky's is also untrue. The text of the *Humanité* article reads as follows:

> J'ai ensuite demandé au consul de nous prêter une aide matérielle, lui disant que nous lui rendrions l'argent prêté aussitôt que notre situation financière changerait.

> À l'entrevue suivante, la troisième ou la quatrième au consulat, le consul m'informa qu'il était prêt à satisfaire à ma demande et me remit 5.000 roubles.
>
> Il dit qu'il pouvait établir **la liaison** avec Trotsky si je lui remettais une lettre du groupe à Trotsky.

Translated:

> Then I asked the consul to lend us material help and told him that we would return the money borrowed as soon as our financial situation changed.
>
> At the following interview, the third or fourth at the consulate, the consul informed me that he was ready to satisfy my request and gave me 5,000 rubles.
>
> He said that he could establish **the contact** with Trotsky if I gave him a letter from the group to Trotsky.

The first mention in this text of contact with Trotsky is by the consul. Neither the Russian text nor the abbreviated French translation explicitly specifies which party first suggested contact with Trotsky. However, the French text in *Humanité* says "la liaison" – "the contact" – meaning a contact previously mentioned. Since the consul then asks Nikolaev for a letter "from the group to Trotsky" the most obvious interpretation would be that Nikolaev, on behalf of "the group," had asked for the contact with Trotsky.

This passage is identified as an extract from a confession of Nikolayev's of December 20. We know now that it was indeed Nikolaev who, in a part of his December 20 statement not quoted in the indictment, "asked the consul to connect our group with Trotsky." [17]

A little further on Trotsky wrote:

---

[17] See Lenoe Document 69 pp. 341-2. Osmund (Åsmund) Egge, *Zagadka Kirova* (Moscow: ROSSPEN, 2011), 175 quotes these passages in the Russian original.

> The version we have adduced, which unfailingly flows from the indictment itself, if one is able to read it, presupposes consequently that the GPU itself, through the medium of an actual or fake consul, was financing Nikolaiev and was attempting to link him up with Trotsky. This version finds its indirect but very actual confirmation in the fact that all the responsible representatives of the GPU in Leningrad were kicked out immediately after the assassination.

This statement too is false. It is also inconsistent with any logical interpretation of the text of the indictment. In reality the Leningrad NKVD men who were dismissed and later brought to trial were charged with criminal dereliction of duty for failing to protect Kirov. This became known only at the end of January 1935.[18]

Trotsky continued:

> The consul himself was the one to assume the initiative and, while giving Nikolaiev 5,000 roubles on the eve of the terrorist act that was being prepared, he requested a letter addressed to Trotsky.

> The dismissals of the Leningrad NKVD men in early December do not at all support Trotsky's "theory" that "the GPU itself... was financing Nikolaiev." It is clear from the text of the indictment in *Humanité* that it was Nikolaev who asked the consul for money, not the consul who offered it first: "*J'ai ensuite demandé au consul de nous prêter une aide matérielle...*"

Trotsky was evidently betting that his readers would not compare his own article with the text in *Humanité*, much less with the original Russian text of the indictment published in *Pravda* and in newspapers all over the Soviet Union. Trotsky knew what his

---

[18] See Lenoe 436-445.

readers did not: that through his clandestine supporters within the USSR, he really was in contact with the Zinovievite group that had murdered Kirov. Therefore this is yet another "amalgam" of Trotsky's – a version of events he knew to be false. The NKVD (Trotsky calls it by its former name, the GPU) was not financing Nikolaev nor trying to "link him up with Trotsky."

Trotsky's Silence about the Bloc

Towards the conclusion of his second article Trotsky makes the following statement:

> The Soviet authorities were compelled to admit openly that the participation of Zinoviev, Kamenev and others "was not proved": **The official dispatches generally made no mention of me at all.** The indictment refers only to the anxiety of the "consul" to obtain a letter to Trotsky – without drawing any conclusions.

Then Trotsky comments on "the unbelievable tone of *Humanité*."

> The lackeys of *Humanité* write that Trotsky's participation in the murder of Kirov was "proved."

The tone of Duclos' article in *Humanité* might indeed be considered "unbelievable" if, as Trotsky claimed in this article, the only mention of his name was in the passage concerning the unidentified consul.

But Trotsky has concealed from his readers something that anyone who reads the actual article in *Humanité* can see for themselves: numerous references to the bloc of Trotskyists and Zinovievists. The bloc and Trotsky's name is mentioned four times in *Humanité's* summary article about the indictment:

> "Ce groupe se forma sur la base d'un ancien **bloc trotskiste-zinovieviste**." (col. 1)

> "Nikolaiev, au cours de ses depositions, le 13 septembre, confirma qu'il appartenait au groupe d'anciens opposi-

tionels qui faisait un travail contre-révolutionnaire, ajoutant que **«*les membres de ce groupe ralliaient la plateforme du* bloc *trotskiste-zinovieviste.*»** (col. 1)

"L'inculpé Khanik, un des membres actifs de ce groupe, caractérisant ses conceptions «idéologiques et politiques» reconnut que «ces conceptions avaient pour point de départ **la plate-forme du bloc Trotsky-Zinoviev** cherchant de miner l'autorité de la direction acutelle du Parti et à remplacer cette direction par des chefs de notre organisation: Zinoviev, Kamenev et autres qui sont partisans du changement de l'orientation actuelle du Parti.» (col. 1)

"Durant la période 1933-1934 les anciens membres du groupe antisoviétique Zinoviev s'organisèrent à Leningrad en groupe terroriste contre-révolutionnaire illégal, agissant comme tel et se posant comme but de désorganiser la direction du gouvernement soviétique au moyen d'actes terroristes dirigés contre les chefs du pouvoir soviétique et changer ainsi la politique actuelle dans l'esprit de **la plate-forme Zinoviev-Trotsky**..." (col. 4)

In its summary, *Humanité* actually *reduced* the number of such references. The original published Russian text of the indictment contains not four but *six* references to the "Zinoviev-Trotsky" or "Trotsky-Zinoviev" bloc or platform. The term "Trotskyist-Zinovievist bloc" occurs *four* times in the Russian original but only three times in the French version.[19]

Thanks to the materials Broué discovered in the Harvard Trotsky Archive we know that the Soviet-based clandestine Trotskyists

---

[19] *Obvinitelnye materialy po delu podpol'noi kontrrevolutsionnoi gruppy zinov'evtsev.* Moscow: Partizdat TsK VKP(b), 1935. This text was published in *Pravda* on December 27, 1934, just before the December trial. We have put this version online in Russian at
https://msuweb.montclair.edu/~furrg/research/obvin_zak_dec34.html

asked Trotsky's permission to form a bloc with the Zinovievists, the Sten-Lominadze group, Safarov, and other oppositionists.

At the present stage of our discussion we can conclude that it is unlikely that the Zinovievists would have murdered Kirov without the agreement of the Trotskyists in the bloc. The Trotskyists would at the very least have obtained the blessings of their leader, Trotsky, before collaborating with those who were planning the murder.

This conclusion finds confirmation in a pretrial confession of Genrikh Iagoda, NKVD chief during the Kirov investigation and defendant in the March 1938 Moscow Trial, who confessed to being one of the "Right" conspirators in the bloc with the Trotskyists, Zinovievists, and others.

> Он сообщил мне о том, что блок между троцкистами и зиновьевцами окончательно оформлен организацией общего центра, что правые также входят в этот блок, но сохраняют свою самостоятельную организацию и свою особую линию.
>
> Вопрос. Какую свою особую линию?
>
> Ответ. По этому вопросу мы с Енукидзе беседовали довольно долго. Я не могу, конечно, сейчас передать в деталях весь наш разговор, но общий смысл его сводится к следующему.
>
> Троцкисты и зиновьевцы, говорил Енукидзе, слились теперь в одну организацию с единым центром и единой программой. С точки зрения конечных целей, мы, правые, ничего своего, что отделяло нас от троцкистов и зиновьевцев, не имеем. Мы так же, как и они, против генеральной линии партии. Против Сталина.
>
> В борьбе за наши конечные цели, за их осуществление, за приход наш к власти мы признаем все средства борьбы, в том числе и террор против руководства партии и Советского правительства. На этой основе и достигнуто было соглашение правых с центром троцкистско-зиновьевского блока.

Но что отделяет нас от этого блока? В чем особенность нашей линии? Дело в том, что троцкисты и зиновьевцы, подстегиваемые находившимся в изгнании Троцким, торопят с совершением террористических актов. Троцкому за границей, наверное, несладко приходится, и он исходит злобой, брызжет слюной и жаждет крови. Он не дает опомниться своему центру в Союзе, он требует террористических актов против членов ЦК, не считаясь с общей ситуацией в стране и вне ее, не считаясь с тем, что такой оторванный от плана заговора террористический акт ничего конкретного нам не даст, а может стоить нам десятка голов наших людей.

Мы же, правые, говорил Енукидзе, не можем и не хотим пускаться на авантюрные акты, продиктованные больше жаждой мести и злобой, нежели рассудком и расчетом. Это не значит, конечно, что мы против террористических актов, что мы питаем какие-либо симпатии к Сталину и его Политбюро. Нет! Мы, как и троцкисты, полны ненависти и негодования, мы, как и они, готовы к террористическим актам, но на такие акты мы пойдем тогда, когда это совпадет с общим нашим планом. «Над нами не капает, мы не в эмиграции. Все наши люди находятся в Союзе, нас особенно не били. Мы можем хладнокровнее готовиться, готовиться всерьез к захвату власти и имеем свои планы," — закончил Енукидзе.

Translated:

He [Avel' Enukidze] informed me that the bloc between the Trotskyists and the Zinovievists was conclusively formed by the organization of a general center, that the Rights also enter into this bloc but have kept their own independent organization and their own special line.

QUESTION: What was their own special line?

ANSWER: Enukidze and I discussed this question for quite a long time. Of course, I cannot now relate our whole conversation in detail but its general sense comes down to the following:

The Trotskyists and Zinovievists, said Enukidze, have now entered into one organization with a single center and a single program. From the viewpoint of our final aims we Rights have nothing special that divides us from the Trotskyists and Zinovievists. Like them, we are also against the general line of the Party. Against Stalin.

In the struggle for our final aims, for bringing them into being, for our attaining power, we recognized all means of struggle, including also terror against the Party leadership and the soviet government. On this basis the agreement of the Rights was reached with the center of the Trotskyist-Zinovievist bloc.

But what separates us from this bloc? In what does the special nature of our line consist? **The fact is this: the Trotskyists and Zinovievists are spurred on by Trotsky who finds himself in exile and so they are in a hurry to accomplish terrorist acts. No doubt it is not easy for Trotsky abroad and he expresses malice, foams at the mouth, and thirsts for blood. He does not permit his center in the Soviet Union to think it over; he demands terrorist acts against members of the CC and does not consider the general situation inside and outside the country,** does not consider the fact that such a terrorist act, in isolation from the plan of the conspiracy, will not yield us any concrete result, and might cost us a dozen of our people's heads.

But we, the Rights, said Enukidze, cannot permit and do not wish to permit adventurist acts dictated more by a thirst for revenge and malice than by sound judgment and reason. Of course that does not mean that we are against terrorist acts, that we harbor any sympathy towards Stalin and his Politburo. No! We, like the Trotskyists, are full of hatred and indignation; we, like they, are prepared for terrorist acts, but we will have recourse to such acts when they suit our general plan. "We are not in danger, we are not in emigration. All of our people are inside the Soviet Union, we have not taken any serious blows. We can prepare ourselves more calmly, seriously prepare for the seizure of power and have our own plans," – said Enukidze. (Genrikh Iagoda 169-171)

What Iagoda states here is consistent with everything else we know about the bloc and about Trotsky's support for terror. In other passages, Iagoda discusses the bloc's involvement in the Kirov murder in a manner that is consistent with the confessions and indictment in the Kirov murder case of December 1934 and with the confessions, both pretrial and during the trial, of Kamenev and Zinoviev.

We do not know why Trotsky did not wish to acknowledge that there really was a Trotskyist-Zinovievite bloc or that the bloc included other opposition groups. Pierre Broué and Vadim Rogovin, skilled researchers but devoted Trotskyists, suggested that Trotsky told his lies in order to save his followers inside the USSR. But this apologetic explanation makes no sense. If Trotsky had admitted only what the Soviets had already made public he would have put no one in danger who was not already known to the Soviets. Therefore Trotsky could not have been trying to defend his Soviet-based followers or to fool "Stalin" and the NKVD.

Trotsky may have believed that he had to preserve "plausible deniability" in order to fight attempts by the Soviet government to deny him any place of exile. Trotsky may also have believed that denying only *some* Soviet charges – for instance, involvement in terror – while admitting to others like the bloc, would not be credible. Perhaps Trotsky feared that he would lose many of his followers if he were to concede that the Soviet NKVD was telling the truth *some* of the time.

Whatever his reasoning, Trotsky decided to deny everything the Soviets charged him and his followers with, including charges that we now know to be true. Given that the bloc was mentioned prominently in the Kirov indictment and that he had decided to deny everything the Soviet prosecution said, Trotsky could do one of two things. He could quote those parts of the indictment that mentioned the "Trotskyist-Zinovievite bloc" and then deny the existence of such a bloc. Or he could ignore those passages – in effect, act as though there were no such passages in the indictment.

Trotsky chose the latter course of action. In doing so he ran a considerable risk. Anyone who read the article in *Humanité* – let alone the original article in *Pravda* – and compared it with what Trotsky had written would immediately notice Trotsky's failure to even mention, much less to deny, the repeated allegations in the indictment that the Zinovievite terrorists were in a bloc with the Trotskyists.

Any such reader would ask: "Why does Trotsky remain silent about these, the most striking allegations in the indictment?" Once noticed, Trotsky's failure not only to deny the charge of a bloc with the Zinovievite terrorists, but even to mention it – if only to call it "yet another amalgam," etc. – would strike any reader as suspicious. After all, failure to deny a serious charge is often interpreted as a tacit admission.

Trotsky must have believed that the risk of openly discussing and denying the Trotskyist-Zinovievite bloc was greater than that of simply passing over it in silence. This suggests that he was writing with a sympathetic, even credulous, readership in mind, or at least one favorably predisposed towards anti-Stalin propaganda, one that would be unlikely to compare the *Humanité* or *Pravda* articles with Trotsky's account. *It seems clear that Trotsky's lies were aimed above all at duping his own followers.*

This is also suggested by his habit of inserting into his writings attacks on Stalin in the form of gratuitous and unverified remarks. Two examples occur in the first of his two essays here. Towards the end of this essay Trotsky makes the following claim:

> В 1926 году Н. К. Крупская, примкнувшая тогда, вместе с Зиновьевым и Каменевым, к левой оппозиции, говорила: "еслиб жив был Ленин, он сейчас, наверное, сидел бы у ГПУ в тюрьме."

Translated:

> In 1926, N.K. Krupskaya, who along with Zinoviev and
> Kamenev then adhered to the Left Opposition, said,
> "Were Lenin alive, he would most assuredly be in a GPU
> prison."

It would be difficult to prove that Krupskaya did not make this
statement. The burden of proof is on Trotsky to prove she did. Besides, it is more than unlikely. In 1926 not a single Oppositionist
had been imprisoned – not Zinoviev, not Kamenev, not Trotsky,
nor any of their supporters. No matter how opposed Krupskaya
was to Stalin's political line in 1926, the idea that she could have
said that Lenin would have been in prison is not credible.

Moreover, no one else had any independent knowledge of this
purported remark. Boris Bazhanov, who worked from 1923 as Stalin's secretary until he fled the USSR in 1928, published the first
volume of his strongly anti-Stalin memoirs, *I Was Stalin's Secretary*, in Paris in 1930. Bazhanov recorded many insulting rumors
about Stalin. But this one only gets into his book in editions published after the French edition of Trotsky's biography *Staline*,
which Bazhanov credits as his source, therefore after 1948:

> В своем секретариате Сталин не стеснялся, и из
> отдельных его фраз, словечек и интонаций я ясно видел,
> как он на самом деле относится к Ленину. Впрочем, это
> понимали и другие, например, Крупская, которая немного
> спустя (в 1926 году) говорила: "Если бы Володя жил, то он
> теперь сидел бы в тюрьме" (свидетельство Троцкого, его
> книга о Сталине, франц. текст, стр. 523).

Translated:

> In his Secretariat Stalin did not hold back and from some
> of his phrases, remarks, and intonations I saw clearly
> what he really thought of Lenin. Moreover, others un-
> derstood this too, for example, Krupskaya, who said a lit-
> tle later (in 1926): "If Volodia were alive he would now

be in prison" (according to Trotsky in his book about Stalin, French edition, p. 523). [20]

An otherwise unattested anecdote such as this one would be believed only by persons who were accustomed to accepting Trotsky's unsupported statements at face value – that is, by Trotskyists.

Trotsky also stated the following as fact:

> During the last two years of his life, Lenin saw in the bureaucracy the principal danger to the revolution and in Stalin the most consummate representative of this danger. Lenin fell ill and died during a feverish preparation of the struggle against the Stalinist apparatus.

This is not true either. There is no evidence of any struggle by Lenin "against the Stalinist apparatus." That was true at the time, and we can confirm it today, since the publication of the relevant documents of Lenin's last year of life since 1989. Unlike the previous remark which, in theory at least, *might* have been uttered by Lenin privately to Trotsky alone, no "feverish preparation" of struggle "against the Stalinist apparatus" could have been kept secret.

This is part of Trotsky's attempt to portray himself as Lenin's rightful successor, to counter Stalin's similar claim that *he* was Lenin's rightful successor.[21] The genuineness of the documents called "Lenin's Testament" has been called into serious question by research based upon the originals.[22] But even if they are genu-

---

[20] See Bazhanov, *Vospominaniia byvshego sekretaria Stalina* ("Memoirs of Stalin's former secretary"), Moscow 1990, Chapter 7; online at http://www.hrono.ru/libris/lib_b/bazhan07.php The French edition of Trotsky's biography of Stalin was published by Grasset (Paris) in 1948.

[21] For a brief discussion of these issues, translations of some of the relevant documents, and references to others, see Furr, *Khrushchev Lied* pp. 11-19 and 232-239.

[22] The main study of this question is the monumental work by V.A. Sakharov, *"Politicheskoe zaveshchanie" Lenina. Real'nost' istorii i mify politiki.* Moscow:

ine, as was believed at the time, Lenin trusted Stalin – and, apparently, only him – enough to ask Stalin alone to give him poison if he, Lenin, should find the pain of his illness unbearable.

Conclusion

The major finding of our study is dramatic. Trotsky did not only deny the bloc of Trotskyists, Zinovievists, Rightists, and other oppositionists, the very evidence of whose real existence was discovered by Pierre Broué in the Harvard Trotsky Archive. He denied his contacts with Zinoviev, Kamenev, Piatakov, and Radek. He also denied accusations made at the Moscow Trials that he had had contact with still other oppositionists, contacts that Broué has verified.

These accusations were central to all three Moscow trials. This means *that not just Trotsky's essays and other discussions of the Kirov murder but all of Trotsky's essays about the Moscow Trials contain deliberate falsifications.*

Once Trotsky had embarked on the practice of declaring that all the evidence in the Kirov assassination, and then in all the future prosecutions of former oppositionists, was faked from beginning to end, there was no turning back. To admit that he had lied would have done more damage to his movement and his credibility than admitting even a part of the truth from the beginning. Unwilling to risk the consequences, it is only logical that Trotsky would stick to this story – that it was Stalin who had fabricated everything.

This means that Trotsky spent the rest of his life repeating and elaborating a picture of the Moscow Trials and of Stalin that he knew to be, at least in significant part, a lie of his own making. Beginning no later than his essay on the Kirov assassination in late

---

Izdatel'stvo Moskovskogo universiteta, 2003. A very short summary by the author is *Podlog zaveshchania vozhdia. Kto avtor?* Available at a number of internet sites including http://stalinism.narod.ru/vieux/saharov.htm

December 1934 Trotsky concocted a series of "amalgams" to the effect that the trials were nothing more than frame-ups by Stalin, the NKVD, and the Prosecutor.

Trotsky knew what he wrote was not the truth but his own fabrication. His followers and the broader readership of his articles in the mainstream press did *not* know this.

A devoted Trotskyist all his life, Pierre Broué shrank from drawing the obvious conclusions from his own discovery that Trotsky had lied about the bloc and other contacts with oppositionists. For example, Broué did not reconsider the two volumes that the Dewey Commission published. How likely is it that the commission would have found Trotsky "Not Guilty"[23] if its members had known that Trotsky really had been in a bloc with the Zinovievists and Rightists; that he really had been in secret contact with Zinoviev, Kamenev, Radek, and Piatakov, whom he had publicly excoriated, and with others whom he had denied contacting?

Still, Broué continued to defend the Commission and its findings as though the documents he himself had discovered in the Trotsky Archives did not exist.[24] I discuss the Dewey Commission in *The Fraud of the Dewey Commission* and in the final chapters of *Trotsky's 'Amalgams.'*

Even so, Broué realized that these discoveries would necessitate a complete revision of the conventional anticommunist and Trotskyist view of the Moscow Trials:

> I think that the new data concerning the "Opposition bloc," the organization of two Communist blocs of Oppositions, the attempt to unify the Communist Opposition, *definitively*

---

[23] The title of the Dewey Commission's report is *Not Guilty. Report of the Commission of Inquiry into the Charges Made Against Leon Trotsky in the Moscow Trials*, John Dewey, chairman. New York, London, Harper & Brothers, 1938.
[24] See Broué, "L'historien devant la vie. Charles A. Beard et les procès de Moscou." CahLT 19 (1984), 68-77. B

> *destroys all the legends and preconceived ideas about an all-*
> *mighty, blood-thirsty, machiavelian* [sic - GF] *Stalin.*
> (Broué POS 110.)

This is a dramatic statement from a famous, lifelong Trotskyist scholar. It is completely ignored by all Trotskyists today, as well as by virtually all mainstream scholars of the Stalin period. It appears that, like Trotsky himself, they are afraid to concede that *any* part of the Moscow Trials testimony was true. As I have shown in *Trotsky's 'Amalgams'* and in *The Moscow Trials as Evidence*, to do so would be to open a "Pandora's box," a cascade of other discoveries that destroys what I have called the "anti-Stalin paradigm," an essential part of which is that the Moscow Trials were frame-ups of innocent defendants.

Trotsky and Anticommunism

Trotsky has sometimes been called an anticommunist. It is worth recalling this epithet in light of the facts uncovered in this essay.

On the one hand, Trotsky evidently considered himself to be a true communist and his movement the true communist movement. In that sense, he was not an anticommunist as that term is normally understood.

However, one understanding of "anticommunist" is someone who deliberately fabricates false tales of terrible crimes which he then blames on communists. This is the sense in which it is logical to call Nikita Khrushchev's "Secret Speech" "anticommunist." It was filled with deliberate falsehoods. It provided ammunition, grist for the mills, of pro-capitalist anticommunists.

In the long run, Trotsky's "amalgams," like those of Khrushchev, were more effective than similar lies invented or spread abroad by opponents of communism.[25] Trotsky and Khrushchev had spent

---

[25] For a sample of Khrushchev's lies about Stalin see Furr Khrushchev Lied.

decades as leading communists themselves. Their "revelations" – for such they claimed their deliberate lies to be – had far more credibility than those of overtly pro-capitalist propagandists.

It appears that Trotsky was the very first writer to characterize the Soviet Union as "totalitarian."[26] Certainly it was Trotsky who put this term in use on the Left. Prior to Trotsky's use of the word in his "amalgams" about the Moscow Trials the word "totalitarian" simply meant a one-party state – something that Trotsky himself had advocated.

Trotsky extended the use of the word "totalitarian" to accommodate his "amalgam" that Stalin had fabricated all the charges against the former oppositionists in all the trials, as well as all of the confessions. Trotsky *knew* that this was not so. He knew that a number -- perhaps many, perhaps even all – the charges against and statements of the defendants, including those against and by his own followers, were true. But he *pretended* that they were all grotesque fabrications, and shouted that falsehood to all the world.

Trotsky's term "amalgam" has become common usage in anticommunist Soviet historiography, a term regularly employed by historians as though it described an established practice on Stalin's part. Witness the following quotation from Oleg Khlevniuk, a prominent anticommunist historian of the Stalin period:

> As in other political affairs of the Stalinist era, the Syrtsov-Lominadze case was, to use Trotsky's apt characterization of the 1936-38 show trials, "an amalgam," a peculiar combination of real facts and falsifications.[27]

---

[26] See IUrii Fel'shtinskii, Georgii Cherniavskii, *Lev Trotskii. Vrag No.1. 1929-1940*. Moscow: Tentrpoligraf, 2013, 116; 195-6.

[27] Oleg V. Khlevniuk, "Stalin, Syrtsov, Lominadze: Preparations for the 'Second Great Breakthrough.'" *The Lost Politburo Transcripts. From Collective Rule to Stalin's Dictatorship*. Ed. Paul R. Gregory and Norman Naimark. Stanford, CA: Hoover Institution (2008), 79.

In reality, it does describe an established practice – but by Trotsky rather than by Stalin.

Not the least of the conclusions we may draw from the discovery of Trotsky's "amalgams" is this: that there is no obvious limit to them. We have established that Trotsky's essay on the Kirov assassination was full of lies, one after the other. Some were obvious, if anyone had bothered to check them. Others, involving the truth about Trotsky's bloc with the Zinovievists, Rights, and others, were closely guarded secrets, known only to Trotsky, his son, and one of his most loyal secretaries, Jean van Heijenoort.

In the present chapter, I have suggested that the fact that Trotsky lied in claiming that Zinoviev and Kamenev were falsely charged with plotting the restoration of capitalism is consistent with the hypothesis that Trotsky really did collaborate with the Germans and Japanese.

This suggests that we should take a fresh look at the allegation that Trotsky collaborated with the Germans and Japanese. We know that Trotsky lied when he claimed that he would never form a bloc with Zinoviev and Kamenev, and also lied when he ridiculed the idea that he could ever have recourse to "terror," i.e. assassination. Yet we know that he did both of these things.

As it turns out, there can be no doubt that Trotsky did indeed collaborate with both the German fascist and Japanese militarists. I have previously attempted to gather and study the Soviet evidence that Trotsky collaborated with Germany and Japan. Now there is even less reason to question that Soviet evidence than we had before. I have completed one book on this subject (Furr, *Leon Trotsky's Collaboration with Germany and Japan*), and will have much more evidence in future books.

Just as we have discovered that Trotsky was lying, it turns out that, in each case where we can check, Soviet prosecutor Vyshinsky and the Moscow Trial defendants were telling the truth. In *Trotsky's 'Amalgams'* and *The Moscow Trials As Evidence* I examine other

Moscow Trial allegations that Trotsky denied. Likewise, now that we know Trotsky attacked Zinoviev, Kamenev, and Radek to cover up his continuing contacts with them, it would be worthwhile to examine whether Trotsky also remained in contact with others with whom he had once been in open alliance but later supposedly broke with, like POUM[28] leader Andrés Nin.

---

[28] This is the common acronym for Partido Obrero de Unificación Marxista – Spain.

Chapter 3. Trotsky and the Charge of "Armed Intervention"

Introduction

Living in France at the time, Leon Trotsky followed the events connected with the Kirov assassination in *Humanité*, daily newspaper of the French Communist Party.[1] *Humanité* covered the Kirov murder case closely, often summarizing articles in *Pravda* and *Izvestia* supplemented by summary and analysis written by their own staff. Sometimes *Humanité* printed translations of important documents verbatim or in long excerpts.

By consulting the pages of *Humanité* and supplementing them with copies of the two Moscow papers, I have read the same articles that Trotsky read and have compared his coverage of the Kirov case with that of his sources. In doing this I have discovered a number of instances where Trotsky falsified the contents of the articles on the Kirov murder and investigation. One of these instances of falsification concerns Trotsky's allegation that Zinoviev and his close associate Lev Kamenev had been charged with planning "armed intervention."

Trotsky's allegations

Trotsky wrote about the supposed accusation of "armed intervention" in two issues of his publication, *Biulleten' Oppozitsii* (in English, "Bulletin of the Russian Opposition") I reproduce Trotsky's words below:

---

[1] Trotsky's writings on the Kirov murder cite *Humanité* and, once, *Le Temps*, as does Sedov in the *Livre rouge* (Red Book). Trotsky occasionally quotes *Pravda* and *Izvestia* in a manner that suggests he had quick access to them.

B.O. #42 February 1935:

Первые правительственные сообщения и официальные статьи после ареста московской группы старых большевиков гласили, что Зиновьев-Каменев и их друзья поставили себе целью «восстановление капиталистического строя," и стремились вызвать иностранную «военную интервенцию» (через посредство... латышского консула!). Ни один серьезный человек не поверил этому, разумеется.

Лакеи Сталина, выступающие под именем «вождей» Коминтерна, не устают, однако, твердить, что Зиновьев, Каменев и др. «сами признали свои преступления." Какие? Подготовку реставрации капитализма? подготовку военной интервенции?

Допустим, что критика Зиновьева неправильна. Признаем даже за лакеями право считать направленную против них критику «преступной." Но причем же тут все-таки «реставрация капитализма» и «военная интервенция»? Какая связь между требованием более революционной политики против буржуазии и программой восстановления буржуазного режима? Где тут здравый смысл? Он полностью погребен под чудовищными извержениями подлости!

Translated:

The first government communique and official articles after the arrest of the Moscow group of Old Bolsheviks said that Zinoviev-Kamenev and their friends had taken as their aim "the restoration of the capitalist system" and they were trying to provoke "armed intervention" from abroad (by the intermediacy of a consul- from Latvia!). No serious person could believe it; that is understood.

...

Stalin's lackeys, who cover themselves with the name of "leaders" of the Communist International, don't, however, recoil at the assertion that Zinoviev, Kamenev and

the others "have themselves admitted their crimes."
Which ones? Preparation of the restoration of capitalism? Preparation of armed intervention?

...

Let us admit that Zinoviev's criticism was false. Let us
even grant that the lackeys were right to judge criticism
directed against them "criminal. " But are we to see in
that the "restoration of capitalism" and "armed intervention"? What connection is there between the demand for
a more revolutionary policy against the bourgeoisie and
a program for "the restoration of a bourgeois regime"?
Where has common sense gone? It is completely buried
beneath a monstrous defecation of infamy.[2]

B.O. #43 April 1935:

> В правительственном сообщении, как и в бесчисленных
> статьях «Правды» заключалось, как известно, прямое и
> категорическое утверждение, что Зиновьев и Каменев
> **ставили себе целью** реставрацию капитализма и
> **военную интервенцию.**
>
> - «Заметки журналиста. Как сталинцы подрывают мораль
> Красной армии.»
>
> Сейчас Майский, в сане посла, обвиняет «зиновьевцев» и
> «троцкистов» в **стремлении вызвать военную
> интервенцию** для реставрации капитализма...
>
> - «Рабочее государство, термидор и бонапартизм
> (Историко-теоретическая справка)»

---

[2] "Письмо американским друзьям." (Letter to American Friends)
http://web.mit.edu/fjk/www/FI/BO/BO-42.shtml ; Trotsky, "Everything
Gradually Falls Into Place." WLT 1934-1935 223-228. (WLT). Originally in B.O.
#42.

Так скажут, вероятно, сталинцы и прибавят на всякий случай, что мы переменили позицию, дабы легче **вызвать военную интервенцию.**

- http://web.mit.edu/fjk/www/FI/BO/BO-43.shtml

Translated:

In the government communique as well as in numerous articles in *Pravda* there was, as is well known, the direct and categorical assertion that Zinoviev and Kamenev *had as their goal the restoration of capitalism and military intervention...*[3]

Today Maisky, in the rank of ambassador, accuses "Zinovievists" and "Trotskyists" of striving to **provoke military intervention** in order to restore capitalism...[4]

...

This will probably be said by Stalinists, who will add for good measure that we have changed our position in order the more easily **to provoke military intervention.**

Trotsky's "Amalgam"

Trotsky did not give any specific references to the "first government communiqué" – in Russian the word is in the plural, *soobshcheniia*, "communiqués" – or "numerous" "official" articles "in *Pravda*" or anywhere else. This is understandable, for there were none to give. These statements of Trotsky's are false. Zinoviev, Kamenev, and others in the "Moscow Center" who were to be tried in mid-January 1935 were not charged with planning "armed

---

[3] "Notes of a Journalist." WLT 1934-1935 323-238, at 327. Originally in B.O. #43. Italics in original.
[4] "The Workers' State, Thermidor and Bonapartism." WLT 1934-1935 240-261, at 251. Originally in B.O. #43.

intervention" any more than they were with the "restoration of capitalism."[5] Trotsky was lying.

I have searched all the issues of *Humanité*, the newspaper of the French Communist Party that was Trotsky's source of information about what the Russian press was publishing. I have reproduced below all the passages where "armed" or "foreign intervention," or language to that effect, are cited in any articles dealing with the Kirov Assassination or its aftermath, including the arrests of Zinoviev, Kamenev and others. Zinoviev, Kamenev, and others in the "Moscow Center" are not accused in any of them.

Humanité Dec. 28 p. 1 col. 6 bottom:

EN 3e PAGE

A Leningrad, les adhérents du groupe étaient en liaison avec le consul d'une puissance capitaliste et escomptaient que l'assassinat de Kîrov provoquerait une **intervention étrangère.**

André Marty article, p. 2 col. 1:

« L'instruction a établi que le groupe n'espérant pas que le meurtre de Kirov servirait de signal à un mouvement intérieur, du pays contre le Parti communiste de l'U. R. S. S. et contre le pouvoir soviétique, comptait sur l'aide directe du dehors, sur **l'intervention de l'armée** et sur l'appui de certains Etats étrangers »

Article on Kirov indictment p. 3 col. 3

Aidés par l'étranger!

---

[5] See Chapter 4 of this book on the "restoration of capitalism" charge.

Cependant, ne comptant pas sur la réalisation de telles actions à « l'intérieur du pays », le groupe TABLAIT DIRECTEMENT SUR L'AIDE « DU DEHORS ," SUR **L'INTERVENTION ARMEE** ET L'AIDE DE CERTAINS ETATS ETRANGERS.

L'espoir de **l'intervention** comme moyen unique de renverser le pouvoir soviétique caractérise nettement le point de vue de l'inculpé Nikolaiev qui ne le cachait pas à ses amis intimes.

L'instruction a établi que Nikolaiev, conformément à un accord préalable avec Kotolynov, a rendu visite à plusieurs reprises à un certain consul de Leningrad...

Humanité Dec. 29 p. 3 col. 2:

« Détail caractéristique les anciens partisans de Zinoviev, qui basaient tous leurs plans antisoviétiques sur le secours de la bourgeoisie internationale par la voie de « **l'intervention** ," après avoir noué des relations avec le consul étranger, essayent maintenant, par son intermédiaire de se lier avec la contrerévolution.

Humanité Dec. 31 1934 p. 3 col. 5

Les *Isvestia* écrivent dans un éditorial « La sentence qui a frappé les assassins de Kirov est l'expression directe (le la volonté de millions de travailleurs remplis d'indignation et d'une haine profonde envers les terroristes fascistes, restes de l'opposition de Zinoviev, qui, s'étant assuré que leur activité antisoviétique ne peut pas trouver de sympathie dans les masses, sont entrés; non seulement dans la voie de la terreur, mais ont misé sur **l'intervention de l'étranger**. Rien ne peut désorganiser le pouvoir soviétique ni arrêter la marche triomphale du socialisme. »

Humanité Jan. 8 1935 p. 2 col. 1:

C'est Nikolaiev qui parle. « Le groupe tablait directement sur l'aide dit dehors, sur **l'intervention armée** et l'aide de certains Etàts étrangers. »

Humanité Jan. 8 1935 p. 3 col. 7:

Les terroristes et leurs liaisons LE CONSUL COMPLICE DES ASSASSINS DE KIROV FUT L'ALLIE DES BLANCS ET L'HOMME DE HITLER

Moscou (Du notre correspondant particulier).

– On sait que le consul de Lettonie, qui eut contact avec les terroristes révolutionnaires et qui est considère comme complice des assassins de Kirov, a été rappelé par son gouvernement, et l'ambassadeur de ce pays en U.R.S.S. a pris connaissance des pièces de l'instruction. L'activité du consul en question ne fut nullement une activité diplomatique: elle comprenait une aide pécuniaire aux terroristes contre-révolutionnaires, la participation à la préparation de leur fuite à l'étranger, le concours à l'introduction d'autres terroristes en U.R.S.S. et la préparation d'une situation facilitant **une intervention antisoviétique armée.**

Or, chacun comprend qu'une intervention ne se fait pas par de petits Etats: même dans le cas où les forces armées de pareils Etats envahissent le territoire d'un grand Etat, elles jouent seulement le rôle d'éclaireurs pour les armées de puissances beaucoup plus importantes, dont elles remplissent la mission militaire, politique et sociale.

Il n'est donc pas difficile de supposer que les derniers actes du diplomate si étrange de ce petit Etat cachaient des forces de beaucoup plus d'envergure pour le compte desquelles il travaillait en réalité.

The Charge of "Armed Intervention"

The accusation of attempting to provoke, counting upon, or hoping for "armed" or "foreign" "intervention" was not applied to Zinoviev, Kamenev, or others of the "Moscow Center" at all. No Soviet documents charge Zinoviev, Kamenev, and the other Old Bolsheviks arrested and tried together with them with planning, counting on, etc., "armed intervention." It was applied in newspaper articles and by the Soviet courts *only* to the members of the Leningrad Center of Zinovievists who had conspired successfully to murder Sergei Kirov. But even against them it was not applied "officially" in any "government communiqué." It was not mentioned either in the indictment or in the sentence.

Trotsky invented this false story. He must have had some reason for doing so. To discover that reason is the goal of the present chapter.

Beginning with the January 1937 Moscow trial two years later, this same accusation was leveled at Trotsky himself, first by his own followers and then by the Soviet court. Thereafter the accusation of plotting "armed intervention" was repeated and elaborated. This cannot be mere coincidence. There must be some relationship between Trotsky's false claim in 1934 and 1935 that Zinoviev and Kamenev had been accused of plotting "armed intervention" and the public accusations beginning in January, 1937, by the Soviet prosecutor and by Trotsky's followers charging that it was Trotsky himself who was plotting "armed intervention."

In the present chapter I investigate that connection. My hypothesis is as follows: Trotsky suspected that, at some point in the near future, members of the bloc would testify that one aspect of the bloc's activities had been the plotting of an armed intervention. This is in fact what happened, only much later, in 1936-1937.

The only way Trotsky could successfully "predict" that such an accusation would be forthcoming is if he knew that it was true and therefore that one or more of the defendants who were members of the bloc was likely to reveal it.

It's very interesting that Trotsky used the term "amalgam" to describe deliberately false stories that blend fact and fiction, because it was so clearly a projection of his own tactics. He used the truth (that the bloc had been plotting an armed intervention) to tell a lie (that Zinoviev-Kamenev and their friends had already been "falsely" accused of the crime). *At this point, we see a pattern of Trotsky preemptively defending himself/his collaborators against accusations of wrongdoing by "predicting" forthcoming allegations.*

Why Did Trotsky Run the Risk of Discovery?

This threat accounts for Trotsky's lying about the "armed intervention" charge. Trotsky took a considerable risk in telling this lie. It would have been easy for anyone who checked either the Russian newspapers or *Humanité* to see that Trotsky was lying about the accusations against Zinoviev and Kamenev. It is logical to think that he only assumed this risk out of some powerful motive.

Once again, Trotsky composed a false story. By claiming that it was, in fact, Stalin who was guilty of deception, Trotsky created an "amalgam" within an "amalgam." Trotsky continued to derisively repeat the falsehood that Zinoviev and Kamenev were accused of planning "armed intervention" until the April 1935 issue of the B.O. After that, he abandoned it. Unlike the "restoration of capitalism" story, which Trotsky was still repeating at the Dewey Commission testimony in April 1937, his false claim that Zinoviev and Kamenev were charged with plotting "armed insurrection" disappears from his writing after April 1935. (I discuss Trotsky's "restoration of capitalism" "amalgam" in the next chapter.)

In the case of the "Zinovievite-Trotskyite bloc" story, we know why Trotsky repeated his falsehood. Such a bloc did exist and Trotsky decided to deny it completely. This decision forced Trotsky to concoct a different version of the Kirov murder – one he knew to be false – and foist it on the world in order to conceal the existence of the bloc. Trotsky argued tirelessly that the story of the bloc was an invention, an "amalgam" of Stalin's, when he knew that in reality it was he himself who was composing an "amalgam." It was Trotsky, not "Stalin," i.e. the Soviet prosecution, who was lying.

The clandestine Zinovievists who had been arrested for the Kirov murder had started to confess and had named their leader, Zinoviev. It was a safe guess that soon they would also name Trotsky, whose followers were in the bloc with the Zinovievists. We know from the Harvard Trotsky Archive that Trotsky had given his approval for the formation of this bloc. Therefore, Trotsky "predicted" that his name would come up in connection with the Kirov investigate. Sure enough, it did.

In the next chapter, I suggest that the same logic holds in the case of the "restoration of capitalism" "amalgam." There I show that the "restoration of capitalism" story more or less accurately reflected the economic plan that Trotsky had been proposing since 1930. It also reflected the "Riutin Platform," which was really the platform of the whole bloc of Zinovievists, Trotskyists, and Rightists. In addition, we have evidence from the January 1937 and March 1938 Moscow Trials testimony that Trotsky was instructing the leaders of the clandestine Trotskyist group in the Soviet Union that a reversion towards capitalism would be the price of cooperation of the capitalist powers, especially Germany and Japan, in connection with the overthrow of the Stalin regime.

As in the case of the "Zinovievite-Trotskyite bloc," "name of Trotsky" and "restoration of capitalism" "amalgams," once we realize that this "armed intervention" story is false, we are left to wonder why Trotsky chose to tell this lie and to tell it repeatedly. Why did he fabricate false accusations instead of simply dealing with the real ones? Trotsky must have thought that he had much to lose if he did not tell this lie.[6]

---

[6] I use the word "lie" because Trotsky deliberately misled his followers, the principal readers of the B.O. and of his other essays.

Trotsky's strategy: "Expose the scheme in advance."

In the previous chapter I examined Trotsky's reactions to the Kirov murder and discussed his strategy of pretending to "predict" that which he knew or could reasonably expect would follow:

> There is only one way to forestall en route the amalgams that are in preparation: *Expose the scheme in advance.* The Stalinists are trying to mold the public opinion of the world police towards expulsions, extraditions, arrests and other more decisive measures. The Leninists must prepare the public opinion of the world proletariat for these possible events. In this case, as in others, it is necessary to speak out openly about what is; that is also the aim of the present article.

Trotsky restated this strategy in his final speech to the Dewey Commission in April 1937:

> The author of these lines and his closest co-thinkers followed attentively the intrigues and provocations of the GPU, and **in advance**, on the basis of particular facts and symptoms, **warned time and again,** in letters as well as in the press, **against Stalin's provocative plans and against amalgams in preparation**. (CLT 486)

I propose that the only way Trotsky could have thought that his mention of the accusation in a newspaper article presaged an "official" accusation to come was if that accusation were true.

This time Trotsky's attempt "to expose the scheme in advance" misfired somewhat. No accusation that Zinoviev and Kamenev had been relying upon "armed intervention" surfaced during the Kirov murder investigation, indictment, trial, and sentencing, nor in the articles or indictment concerning the arrests and trial of Zinoviev, Kamenev, and their followers in the "Moscow Center."

Still, Trotsky must have calculated that the "armed intervention" allegation might come to the fore sooner or later. Trotsky could not prevent this from happening. The only thing he could do was to "get out in front of" the accusation by claiming that he had already "exposed the scheme in advance." As I say in the previous chapter, we know that this was his strategy in "predicting" that his own name would surface during the investigation of the Kirov murder by Zinovievist members of the bloc.

In the present case, my hypothesis was as follows: Trotsky calculated that future confessions would include the charge of "armed insurrection." This is what led Trotsky to anticipate this accusation by "predicting" it.

There are a number of reasons Trotsky might have believed that the "armed intervention" accusation would be forthcoming:

* Trotsky could have known that Zinoviev and Kamenev had been planning for "armed intervention," and therefore that their followers would probably expose this fact.

* Trotsky could have known that the Rights, who were also a part of the bloc, were planning for "armed intervention," and therefore their followers too would probably expose the fact.

If any of the Zinovievists or Rights confessed, they would certainly inculpate the Trotskyists and Trotsky himself. In either of these cases, the Trotskyists, as a constituent part of the bloc, would have known about and agreed to this tactic. That would mean that Trotsky himself must have at least approved it.

In fact, we have good evidence

* from the Moscow Trials transcripts;

* from Marshal Semion Budyonny's letter to Marshal Voroshilov;

* from the full transcript of the trial of Marshal Mikhail Tuk-hachevsky and seven other high-ranking Soviet military leaders, a transcript only declassified and released to the public in May, 2018;[7]

* and from Piatakov's recently-declassified NKVD file,

that Trotsky himself actively promoted armed intervention against the USSR. I discuss the first two sources in the present volume and will examine Piatakov's NKVD file in a future volume. [8]

* Trotsky himself had been advocating "armed intervention" to his supporters in the USSR. The Zinovievists and Rights would have known about this. Even if they did not know about it, the Zino-vievists had named Trotsky. So the arrests of yet more Trotskyists would have been imminent and *they* might well reveal that Trot-sky was relying on "armed intervention."

The evidence now available suggests the last scenario is the most likely. I will present the evidence that supports this hypothesis. But in any case, Trotsky's "amalgam," or lie, about "armed inter-vention" must be accounted for. In the rest of this essay, I will give:

* evidence that Trotsky was planning "armed intervention" as a means to gain power in the USSR;

* evidence that corroborates or confirms this evidence;

* a consideration of other possible hypotheses that might be cited to explain Trotsky's repeated lie that Zinoviev and Kamenev were accused of plotting armed intervention.

---

[7] I will examine this transcript in a future study.
[8] My Moscow colleague Vladimir L. Bobrov and I plan to devote an entire study to the Tukhachevsky Affair in the near future.

Evidence: The January 1937 Moscow Trial

We have evidence from the January 1937 and March 1938 Moscow Trials testimony that Trotsky was instructing the leaders of the clandestine Trotskyist group in the Soviet Union that a reversion to capitalism might well be the price of cooperation of the capitalist powers, especially Germany and Japan. Additionally, the Trotskyist leaders on trial also testified that they might have to rely on the military might of capitalist powers in order to seize power.

In his opening statement at the 1937 Trial, Andrei Y. Vyshinsky, the Soviet prosecutor, summarized pretrial testimony by Karl Radek:

> The main task which the parallel centre set itself was **the forcible overthrow of the Soviet government** with the object of changing the social and state system existing in the U.S.S.R. L.D. Trotsky, and on his instructions the parallel Trotskyite centre, aimed at **seizing power with the aid of foreign states** with the object of restoring capitalist social relations in the U.S.S.R. (5)

> Proceeding from this program, L. D. Trotsky and his accomplices in the parallel centre entered into negotiations with agents of foreign states with the object of overthrowing the Soviet government with the aid of **armed intervention**. (6)

> The investigation has established that L.D. Trotsky entered into negotiations with one of the leaders of the German National-Socialist Party with a view to **waging a joint struggle against the Soviet Union.**

> L.D. Trotsky and his accomplices in the U.S.S.R. considered it necessary, during the forthcoming war, to adopt an active defeatist position and to do all they could **to assist the foreign interventionists in their fight against the U.S.S.R.**

For example, the accused Piatakov, relating the conversation he had with L. Trotsky in December 1935 near Oslo, testified:

> As regards the war, L.D. Trotsky spoke of this very explicitly. From his point of view, war is inevitable in the near future.
>
> He, Trotsky, considers it absolutely necessary to adopt a distinctly defeatist attitude in this war. He considers that the bloc's coming into power can certainly be hastened by **the defeat of the U.S.S.R. in war**. (Vol. I, p. 258.) (10)

Piatakov's testimony

> I recall that Trotsky said in this directive that without the necessary support from foreign states, a government of the bloc could neither come to power nor hold power. It was therefore a question of arriving at the necessary preliminary agreement with the most aggressive foreign states, like Germany and Japan, and that **he, Trotsky, on his part had already taken the necessary steps in establishing contacts both with the Japanese and the German governments**. (53)
>
> ... later, in the middle of 1935, Sokolnikov himself told me of this step and recounted the conversation in which he had sanctioned **Trotsky's negotiations with the Japanese government**. (53-4)
>
> About the end of 1935 Radek received a long letter—instructions from Trotsky. In this directive Trotsky advanced two possible variants of our coming into power. The first variant was the possibility of our coming into power before a war, and the second variant, during a war. Trotsky visualized the first variant resulting from a concentrated terrorist blow, as he said .... **The second**

variant, which in Trotsky's opinion was the more probable, was a military defeat. (55)

In this connection Trotsky again said that in his opinion war was imminent, that he knew for a fact that it was a question not of, say, a five-year period, but of a short time....The other task was a more practical one: to train cadres for the event of war, that is to say, **to train diversionists and those who would engage in destruction, helpers for the fascist attack on the Soviet Union.** (62)

In connection with the international question Trotsky very emphatically insisted on the necessity of **preparing diversionist cadres**. He rebuked us for not engaging energetically enough in diversive, wrecking and terrorist activities. He told me that he had come to an absolutely definite agreement with the fascist German government and with the Japanese government that they would adopt a favourable attitude in the event of the Trotskyite-Zinovievite bloc coming to power. (64)

First, the German fascists promise to adopt a favourable attitude towards the Trotskyite-Zinovievite bloc and to support it if it comes to power, either in time of war ... (64)

... since Hess and Trotsky had discussed the question of war and a military *coup d'état*, accession to power, that is to say, the defeat of the U.S.S.R.—Hess, of course, quite naturally raised the point: Well, you are fighting over there; while in this case we are a much better organized and a better armed force. It is clear once we negotiate you must go the whole length. **In the event of military attack the destructive forces of the Trotskyite organizations which would act within the country must be co-ordinated with the forces from without acting under the guidance of German fascism.** The diversive and wrecking activity which is being conducted by the

Trotskyite-Zinovievite organization within the Soviet Union must be carried out under the instructions of Trotsky, which are to be agreed upon with the German General Staff.

Towards the end there was talk to the effect that, say, the Trotskyite-Zinovievite bloc comes into power **with the aid of certain external forces, they put us into power**. (65)

The testimony of Trotskyist defendant G.Y. Sokol'nikov addresses the question of "armed intervention" most directly:

VYSHINSKY: And what about the aggressors?

SOKOLNIKOV: We were prepared to come to an agreement with them, the result of which would be that in the course of war and as a result of the defeat of the Soviet Union, the government of the bloc would come to power.

VYSHINSKY: It would therefore be correct to say that you were banking on **help from foreign interventionists?**

SOKOLNIKOV: You see ... perhaps it is something worse ...

VYSHINSKY: I am not speaking of what is worse or of what is better. I am not passing moral judgment. I am establishing facts. I, as the representative of the State prosecution, assert that you were directly staking on **the assistance of foreign aggressors, on the assistance of foreign interventionists**. Is my assertion correct?

SOKOLNIKOV: It is correct that we calculated on the help of foreign aggressors. Interventionists—I would not say. (156)

The Rights Also Confessed To Plotting "Armed Intervention"

Genrikh Iagoda was head of the OGPU and, between 1934 and October 1936, Commissar of Internal Affairs and head of the police force known as the NKVD.[9] Iagoda was arrested at the beginning of March 1937 and began to confess to being an important participant in the conspiracy of the Right oppositionists. In 1997 pretrial confessions of Iagoda were published in a small academic edition in Russia. These confessions are routinely cited as genuine by mainstream scholars of the Soviet period.

Iagoda testifies about the bloc's relations with Germany:

> Помню, что Карахан говорил о двух вариантах соглашения: один, если центр заговора приходит к власти самостоятельно без помощи немцев; второй, если **заговорщикам в их приходе к власти помогут немецкие штыки во время войны**.
>
> При первом варианте речь шла о следующих условиях:
>
> 1. Разрыв СССР договоров о союзе с Францией и Чехословакией.
>
> 2. Заключение военного и экономического союзов с Германией.
>
> 3. Ликвидация Коминтерна.
>
> 4. Предоставление Германии [права] на долголетние концессии источников химического сырья СССР (Кольского полуострова, нефтяных источников и прочее).
>
> 5. Установление в СССР такого политического и экономического строя, который гарантирует германским

---

[9] The initials NKVD indicate the name of the Commissariat (= ministry) itself, "People's Commissariat of Internal Affairs" but are commonly used to refer to the police and investigative section of this large organization. The OGPU became a part of the NKVD in July, 1934.

фирмам полную возможность развития своей частной
инициативы на территории СССР.

При втором варианте, т. е. **при приходе к власти в
военное время при помощи немцев**, оставались в силе
те же условия, плюс какие-то территориальные уступки,
но какие именно я не помню. Об этом должен полнее и
точнее показать сам Карахан.

. . .

Вопрос: А как мыслился приход к власти на случай
войны?

Ответ: Речь шла о восстании наших партий в тылу, аресте
членов правительства **при одновременном открытии
фронта неприятелю заговорщиками из военного
блока**. (198)

Translated:

I recall that Karakhan talks about two variants of the
agreement: one, if the center of the conspiracy should
come to power independently, without the Germans'
help; the second, **if German bayonets were to help the
conspirators to take power during wartime.**

In the first variant, the following conditions would apply:

1. The cancellation by the USSR of agreements about alliance with France and Czechoslovakia.

2. The conclusion of military and economic agreements
with Germany.

3. The liquidation of the Comintern.

4. The presentation to Germany of [rights to] long-term
concessions of sources of chemical resources in the
USSR (the Kola peninsula, petroleum sources, and so
on).

5. The establishment in the USSR of a political and economic system that would guarantee to German compa-
nies the full possibility of development of their private
initiative on the territory of the USSR.

In the case of the second variant, i.e. **in the event [the
bloc] came to power during wartime with German
help**, these same conditions would hold, plus some territorial concessions, but I do not remember exactly what
they were. Karakhan himself should confess about this
more fully and accurately.

. . .

QUESTION: And how was the coming to power in the
case of war imagined?

ANSWER: Through an uprising of our parties in the rear,
the arrest of members of the government **while at the
same time opening the front to the enemy by the
conspirators of the military bloc.**

Nikolai Bukharin, along with Aleksei Rykov, was arrested and imprisoned at the close of the discussion of their cases at the Febru-
ary-March 1937 Plenum of the Central Committee. It has long been
known that Bukharin made his first confession on June 2, 1937. A
copy of that confession, which is still secret in Russia today, is in
the Volkogonov Archive in the National Archives, Washington, DC.
Vladimir Bobrov and I have published it, together with a commentary.[10]

In that first confession, Bukharin testifies about the bloc's, and
specifically Trotsky's, reliance upon armed intervention:

---

[10] Furr and Bobrov, "Nikolai Bukharin's First Statement of Confession in the
Lubianka." *Cultural Logic* 2007. At
http://clogic.eserver.org/2007/Furr_Bobrov.pdf The Russian original, published
in 2007 in the Russian historical journal *Klio* (St Petersburg) is at
https://msuweb.montclair.edu/~furrg/research/furrnbobrov_bukharin_klio07.p
df

In the summer of 1934, I was at RADEK'S apartment when RADEK informed me about TROTSKY'S external political arrangements. RADEK said that **Trotsky, stressing terror, all the same considered the main chance for the arrival in power of the bloc to be the defeat of the USSR in war with Germany and Japan**, and in connection to this was promoting the idea of an agreement with Germany and Japan at the cost of territorial concessions (Ukraine to the Germans, the Far East to the Japanese). (17)

Evidence: Tukhachevsky's confessions

Marshal Mikhail Tukhachevsky was arrested in the fourth week of May 1937. Within two days, he began to make detailed confessions about his conspiracy against the Stalin leadership. Among other matters, he discussed the plans for intervention by foreign powers.

> ... Romm also passed on that it was Trotsky's hope that Hitler would come to power and would support him, Trotsky, in his struggle against Soviet power.[11] (Main 159)

> Round about this time, 1933/1934, Romm visited me in Moscow and told me that he had to pass on Trotsky's new instructions. Trotsky pointed out that it was no longer feasible to restrict our activities to simply recruiting and organizing cadres, that it was necessary to adopt a more concrete programme, that German Fascism

---

[11] Translation by Steven J. Main, "The Arrest and 'Testimony' of Marshal of the Soviet Union M.N. Tukhachevsky (May-June 1937)." *Journal of Slavic Military Studies* 10, 1 (1997), 151-195. Main puts scare quotes around the word "testimony" to show that he doubts that Tukhachevsky made the confession willingly. This is a requirement of those who wish to show their loyalty to the "anti-Stalin paradigm," *de rigeur* in mainstream Soviet history. Main has no evidence whatsoever that the confession is other than it purports to be. I examine the dishonest tactic of "argument by scare quotes" in Kirov, Chapter 4, 87ff.

would render the Trotskyists assistance in their struggle with Stalin's leadership and that the military conspiracy must supply the German General Staff with intelligence data, as well as working hand in glove with the Japanese General Staff, carrying out disruptive activities in the army, prepare diversions and terrorist acts against members of the government. These instructions of Trotsky I communicated to the center of our conspiracy. (Main 160-161)

During the winter of 1935/1936, Piatakov told me that Trotsky had now asked us to ensure the [future] defeat of the USSR in war, even if this meant giving the Ukraine to the Germans and the Primor'ye to the Japanese. In order to prepare the USSR's defeat, all forces, both within the USSR and outside [sic - GF] the USSR would have to be made ready; in particular, Piatakov stated that Trotsky would carry out a decisive struggle to plant his people in the Comintern. Piatakov stated that such conditions would mean the restoration of capitalism in the country... (Main 163)

Thus, developing our platform based on supporting the Rightists in their struggle against the general line of the Party, adding to it, subsequently, Trotskyite slogans, the end result was that the anti-Soviet military Trotskyite conspiracy had embarked on the path of overthrowing Soviet power through a counter-revolution by terror, espionage, diversionary activities, sabotage, defeatist activity [leading to] the restoration of capitalism in the USSR. (Main 163)

In the autumn of 1935, Putna came to my office and handed over a note from Sedov, in Trotsky's name, insisting that I more energetically attract Trotskyite cadres to the military conspiracy and more actively use them. I told Putna to say that this would be done. In addition, Putna told me that Trotsky had established direct links with Hitler's government and the General Staff, and that the center of the anti-Soviet military Trotskyite conspiracy should task itself to prepare defeats on those fronts where the German Army would operate. (Main 166)

As I have already pointed out in the first section, during the strategic military exercises carried out in April 1936, on the question of the operational position of our armies, I exchanged opinions with Yakir and Uborevich. Taking into account Trotsky's directive to prepare for defeat on that front where the Germans would attack, as well as General Rundstedt's instruction to prepare for defeat on the Ukrainian Front ... (Main 185)

Primakov, as quoted in Budyonny's letter to Voroshilov:

Отрицал он это на том основании, что, якобы, ему, ПРИМАКОВУ, ТРОЦКИМ была поставлена более серьезная задача – **поднять в Ленинграде вооруженное восстание,** для чего он ПРИМАКОВ, должен был строго законспирироваться от всех террористических групп, порвать свои связи со всеми троцкистами и правыми и тем самым завоевать авторитет и абсолютное доверие со стороны партии и армейского командования.... В связи **с этим специальным заданием ТРОЦКОГО,** ПРИМАКОВ обрабатывал 25 кавдивизию во главе с командиром дивизии ЗЫБИНЫМ. По его словам, **ЗЫБИН должен был встретить на границе ТРОЦКОГО при овладении повстанцами Ленинградом.**[12]

Translated:

---

[12] "Narodnomu kommisaru Oborony Soiuza SSR Marshalu Sovietskogo Soiuza tov. K.E. Voroshilovu." *Klio* (St Petersburg) No. 2 (2012), 21.

He denied that on the basis that supposedly **he, Primakov, had been entrusted by Trotsky with a more serious task – to raise an armed insurrection in Leningrad**, for which he Primakov must keep himself strictly
apart from any terrorist groups, break his ties with all
Trotskyites and Rights, and at the same time win for
himself authority and absolute trust from the party and
the army command.... **In connection with this special
assignment of Trotsky's**, Primakov had worked on the
25th cavalry division headed by the commander of the
division, Zybin. According to his words **Zybin had been
supposed to meet Trotsky at the border once the re-
bels had taken over Leningrad.**

Liushkov

The testimony of Genrikh Samoilovich Liushkov, NKVD General
and defector in June 1938 to the Japanese, represents some of the
strong evidence from outside of the USSR, and thus beyond the
reach of the NKVD, that confirms the truthfulness of some of the
testimony and charges at the Moscow Trials. Liushkov's remarks
to his Japanese handlers confirm key elements of Tukhachevsky's
confessions. It also confirms the charges at the March 1938 Moscow Trial including, explicitly, Rykov's involvement in the anti-
government conspiracy and the conspiracy of some leading military officers.[13]

Concerning the issue of "armed intervention," Alvin Coox summarized what Liushkov told his Japanese handlers as follows:

> According to Lyushkov, the interrogations of Deribas,
> Zapadni, and Barminski established that in the NKVD
> and the border guard forces, a plot centering on Ga-
> marnik had been fomented. For a long time Deribas had
> been in contact with Rykov and was the latter's 'hidden
> conspirator'. In concert with Lavrenty Lavrentiev (for-

---

[13] Furr Kirov Chapter 17: "Liushkov's Essay," 336-358.

mer First Secretary of the Regional Committee of the
Party until January 1937), with Grigory Krutov (shot in
April 1938), and with the army plotters Sangurski, Ar-
onshtam, and others, Deribas supposedly intended to
conduct a putsch in the Far East and **to reach agreement with the Japanese for help and for combined
operations against the Soviet Union**. (Coox 1, 156)

I also examine Liushkov's disclosures to his Japanese handlers in
Trotsky's 'Amalgams' and *The Moscow Trials as Evidence*.

Evidence: the March 1938 Moscow Trial

Prosecutor Vyshinsky:

> The extensive application of wrecking measures in Uz-
> bekistan was also fully corroborated by the accused IK-
> RAMOV, who testified that the "bloc of Rights and Trot-
> skyites" had set him the following tasks:
>
> > ...a) to make extensive preparations in Uzbekistan
> > for armed insurrection, to be started simultane-
> > ously with the beginning of intervention ... (17)
>
> > ...
>
> GRINKO: ... At the beginning of 1935 I heard from Lyub-
> chenko about the creation in the Ukraine of a national-
> fascist organization, the object of which was to sever the
> Ukraine from the U.S.S.R., and which **counted on receiv-
> ing assistance in the shape of military intervention**
> on the part of those forces and elements with whom I
> had already established personal contact at that time.
> The national-fascist organization also set itself the aim of
> uniting with the "bloc of Rights and Trotskyites," which
> had established contact with the military conspirators.
> (70)

IVANOV: We assembled insurrectionary groups, chiefly around Archangel, so as, **at the moment of intervention**, to cut off communication between Archangel and the central arteries of our country, and thus make it easier for the British to seize this timber region and most valuable port. (124)

IVANOV: ... During this conversation in particular, I asked: where is the intervention, where is the attack on the Soviet Union? Bukharin told me that measures were being taken to induce the fascist countries Japan and Germany to take action without fail in 1937, and the chances of this were good. (127)

KRESTINSKY: This was the question which confronted us, and in our brief conversations with Piatakov we were thinking, we were saying that without help from the outside, that is to say, **without intervention, without armed assistance from outside, we could not manage**, and when I went abroad ...

IKRAMOV: ... Antipov informed me about the German-Japanese orientation and about the connections with the Germans and Japanese. He also told me that there was a military group, and that in the event of war they would act by **opening the front to the attacking forces of the interventionists.** (360)

IKRAMOV: It was during the Congress of Soviets in November or the beginning of December 1936. During the Congress of Soviets I met Bukharin on the staircase; nobody was about, and I asked him about this. He answered in the affirmative, and formulated it as follows: **if there will not be a war just now, if there will not be intervention soon, it is all over with our business.** (361)

BUKHARIN: Tomsky considered it permissible to take advantage of war and preliminary agreements with

Germany. This I opposed by the following arguments, I said that in the first place **if Germany were to intervene in one way or another during the war to help the counter-revolutionary coup**, then, as it always happens, Germany, being rather a strong military and technical factor, would inevitably put her feet on the table and tear up any preliminary agreement which had been concluded. (431)

BUKHARIN: When I asked Tomsky how he conceived the mechanics of the coup he said this was **the business of the military organization, which was to open the front.**

VYSHINSKY: So Tomsky was preparing to open the front?

BUKHARIN: He did not say that.

VYSHINSKY: Yes or no?

BUKHARIN: I asked how he visualized **the mechanism of this intervention.**

VYSHINSKY: Whose intervention?

BUKHARIN: Of certain foreign states. (433)

BUKHARIN: I said that I asked Tomsky: "**How is the mechanism of this intervention visualized?**" He answered: "This is the business of the military organization, which is **to open the front to the Germans.**" (434)

Corroborating evidence

The evidence cited above constitutes *direct* evidence that not only Trotsky but the "Bloc of Rights and Trotskyites" itself, including the Rights, advocated "armed intervention" as a part of a plan for seizing power in the USSR. There is also a good deal of *corroborating* evidence—evidence tending to strengthen or confirm the direct evidence in some way. The subject of the present chapter – Trotsky's lie that Zinoviev and Kamenev were accused of planning "armed intervention" – can itself be considered as corroborating evidence that confirms or strengthens the case that Trotsky conspired with Germany and Japan - a case that I make more fully in *Leon Trotsky's Collaboration with Germany and Japan.*

Piatakov's Face-To-Face Confrontation with Bukharin December 7, 1936

In 2002, the transcript of Iurii Piatakov's "face-to-face" confrontation with Nikolai Bukharin was published in *Voprosy Istorii*, a leading Russian history journal. In it, Piatakov confirms all his previous confessions. He does not specifically mention his charge that Trotsky was conspiring with Germany. If he had done so, that would have been direct, not corroborating, evidence.

Its significance is that not only Nikolai Ezhov, People's Commissar of Internal Affairs (head of the NKVD), but Marshal Kliment Voroshilov, Commissar for Heavy Industry Sergo Ordzhonikidze, and Stalin himself were present. It was never intended for publication.

There is no reason to think Piatakov's statements were "forced," and there is no evidence they were. Bukharin privately told his wife, Anna Larina, about this meeting, as Larina recounted in her memoirs. Bukharin told her that Ordzhonikidze had asked Piatakov repeatedly whether his testimony were "voluntary." Piatakov assured him that it was entirely voluntary.[14]

In his confrontation with Bukharin, Piatakov confirmed that, at their meeting in 1931, Leon Sedov gave him Trotsky's instructions about the formation of a Trotskyist bloc with the Rightists within the USSR, one that was already in the process of formation. We know this independently from Trotsky's and Sedov's own documents in the Harvard Trotsky Archive.

---

[14] Anna Larina. *This I Cannot Forget. The Memoirs of Nikolai Bukharin's Widow.* New York: Norton, 1993, p. 312.

Therefore, in this one instance where we can check Piatakov's confession against information we know to be true from another source, Piatakov was telling the truth. This lends credibility to the rest of Piatakov's statements.[15]

Sokol'nikov and Radek

Just before the end of the USSR, a short excerpt from pretrial confessions by Sokol'nikov and Radek were published. In the course of the pretrial investigation in December 12, 1936, Sokol'nikov testified that Tamekichi Ota, Japanese ambassador to the USSR, asked him, Sokol'nikov, on April 13, 1935, whether he was aware that "Mr. Trotsky has made certain proposals to my government." In the trial transcript, the identity of the country and the ambassador were omitted. In the next volume of the present study I will present evidence that corroborates the validity of Sokol'nikov's testimony that he was approached by the Japanese concerning Trotsky's collaboration with them.[16]

It is not likely that this testimony was "fabricated" – that is, faked – and then the details omitted at the trial itself and in the transcript. Such a charade would have been pointless. Moreover, as we point out in more detail in *Trotsky's 'Amalgams'* and *The Moscow Trials as Evidence*, there has *never* been *any* evidence that the defendants' testimony at the Moscow Trials was "compelled" in any way. All the evidence we have supports the hypothesis that the Moscow Trials defendants *said what they chose to say.*

On December 16, 1936, just four days after this testimony by Sokol'nikov, Georgi Dimitrov wrote about it in his private diary.

---

[15] "Stenogramma ochnykh stavok v TsK VKP(b). Dekabr' 1936 goda. No. 3. Stenogramma ochnoi stavki mezhdu Piatakovym i Bukharinym v Ts.K VKP(b) ot 7 dekabria 1936 goda." *Voprosy Istorii* 4 (2003) 3-12. The "face-to-face confrontation" is on pp. 3-7; the rest of the article is a letter of Bukharin's to Stalin.

[16] See also Furr Evidence. 66-73; Furr, Trotsky's Collaboration, Chapter 1.

Dimitrov copied or summarized a passage that must be at the conclusion of the transcript of this interrogation of Sokol'nikov:

> QUESTION: Thus, the investigation concludes that Trotsky abroad and the center of the bloc within the USSR entered into negotiations with the Hitlerite and Japanese governments with the following terms:
>
> First, to provoke a war by Germany and Japan against the USSR;
>
> Second, to promote the defeat of the USSR in that war and to take advantage of that defeat to achieve the transfer of power in the USSR or [their] government bloc;
>
> Third, on behalf of the future bloc government to guarantee territorial and economic concessions to the Hitlerite and Japanese governments.
>
> Do you confirm this?
>
> REPLY: Yes, I confirm it.[17]

Some pretrial testimony of Radek's likewise confirms his testimony at trial, where crucial details were omitted. I refer the reader to my longer discussion elsewhere.[18]

Conclusion

Trotsky lied in stating that Zinoviev and Kamenev had been charged with "provoking" or otherwise counting on "armed intervention." in order to oust Stalin et al. and bring themselves to power. The question is: Why did he fabricate this particular lie? Why did Trotsky repeatedly make statements that anyone who took the trouble to verify them could readily see were false? Why did he take such a clear risk of exposure?

---

[17] *The Diary of Georgi Dimitrov*, ed. Ivo Banac (Yale U.P., 2003), 43.
[18] Furr Evidence. 66-73.

My hypothesis is that Trotsky told this lie in order to anticipate an accusation that he could reasonably expect to emerge at some point: that he, Leon Trotsky, had been urging his followers to count on the intervention of hostile powers to bring him and the bloc to power. He could reasonably expect this accusation would be made because (a) he had indeed been doing this, and his followers in the bloc knew it; and (b) because others in the bloc – Zinovievists and Rights – not only knew that Trotsky advocated "armed intervention" but were doing so themselves. Hence if they were caught – say, through the confession of one or more of their members – they would have no reason not to inculpate Trotsky too. Because the NKVD had arrested many members of the bloc and on the basis of their confessions was continuing the investigation and arresting more of them, it was likely that, sooner or later, one or more of these men would reveal what Trotsky had been doing. This is, in fact, what happened.

Other possible hypotheses

No single piece or unit of evidence is unequivocal. When viewed individually, in isolation from the whole concatenation of evidence, any piece of evidence can be accounted for in multiple ways. The explanatory power of circumstantial evidence is revealed when multiple pieces of evidence can all be accounted for by only one hypothesis, one single explanatory narrative.[19] In this chapter, I have outlined that hypothesis.

It is important to ask what other hypotheses might be able to account for Trotsky's deliberate lies that Zinoviev, Kamenev, and their followers were planning to "provoke armed intervention" by

---

[19] "In practice, circumstantial evidence can have an advantage over direct evidence in that it can come from multiple sources that check and reinforce each other." "Circumstantial Evidence," Wikipedia, at http://en.wikipedia.org/wiki/Circumstantial_evidence#Validity_of_circumstantial_evidence

a hostile state. Any alternate hypothesis would have to satisfy the same requirements:

* It would have to account for the obvious "coincidence" that, although Trotsky's claim that Zinoviev and Kamenev had been charged with desiring "armed intervention" was false, he himself and other members of the bloc were to be accused of exactly this same crime two years later.

* It would also have to set forth a different yet equally persuasive reason for Trotsky's lie. Trotsky took a considerable risk of being exposed as a liar. If Trotsky had simply criticized and/or ridiculed the real accusations against Zinoviev and Kamenev, without lying about the charges against them, he would have run no such risk. Indeed, he would have been expressing the doubts many people had at the time about who the real murderers of Kirov were. Therefore, we must assume that Trotsky had a very compelling reason to lie in precisely this way.

The hypothesis set forth in the present essay satisfies both of these requirements: it accounts for both the apparent "coincidence" and Trotsky's motive for telling such a blatant lie.

Our hypothesis is strengthened because it suggests that Trotsky was once again relying on his strategy of "exposing the scheme in advance": of feigning to predict an accusation that he knew was likely to be made in the future, since he knew it to be true and also knew that at least one of those in the bloc who knew about it too would be likely to reveal it when arrested and questioned. I have shown that Trotsky employed this tactic on other occasions.

The fact that Trotsky denied the accusations that he was relying on "armed intervention" is not significant. Trotsky would have denied this accusation whether it were true or false. We know the bloc of Trotskyists, Zinovievists, and Rights did exist despite the fact that Trotsky repeatedly and strenuously denied it. Thanks to Broué, Getty, and Holmström, we know that Trotsky lied about other matters as well. Thanks to Getty, we also know that Trotsky's Archive has been "purged," no doubt of incriminating materials.

* * * * *

There is no other reasonable hypothesis that can account for Trotsky's false claim that Zinoviev and Kamenev had been accused of planning an "armed intervention." Moreover, our hypothesis is the most obvious one, the one that would immediately present itself to any objective researcher.

Despite this fact, I predict that our hypothesis will be rejected by some people on political, not evidentiary, grounds. Contemporary historiography of the Soviet Union is dominated by ideological anticommunism. Under the sway of this anticommunism many people refuse to accept any historical explanation, no matter how well it accounts for the evidence, if it tends to make the Moscow Trials testimony appear genuine, or if it fails to reinforce the dominant paradigm of Joseph Stalin as bloodthirsty dictator and falsifier.

This is true of Trotskyist historians as well, who are accepted at the margins of mainstream anticommunist historiography. Typically, Trotskyists are unwilling to consider the possibility that Trotsky lied other than in order to save his followers in the Soviet Union. They are ideologically unwilling to countenance the possibility that Soviet accusations of Trotsky's involvement with German and/or Japan might be accurate despite all the evidence now available to support that conclusion.

I believe that political bias accounts for the fact that the research reported in this paper was not done before this. In another, less politicized field of historical study, some scholar or student would have long ago done what I did: obtain the articles from *Humanité*, *Pravda*, and *Izvestia*, and compared them to what Trotsky wrote. The fact that this has not occurred speaks to the strong political biases that dominate the field of Soviet studies.

The phenomenon of Trotsky's "amalgam" about "armed intervention" should not be ignored, no matter how inconvenient it may be for politically-motivated persons. It has to be accounted for.

It may be that there is another hypothesis that better explains Trotsky's taking the risk he did in lying about Zinoviev and Kamenev being accused of supporting "armed intervention." But until such an alternative hypothesis is shown to account for the evidence better than the one I have proposed here, we must consider this hypothesis as proven by the available evidence.

Chapter 4. Trotsky's Kirov Assassination article – "The Restoration of Capitalism"

"The Restoration of Capitalism"

In his article "On the Kirov Assassination," dated December 30, 1934, which comprises the entire issue #41 of the *Biulleten' Oppozitsii*, Trotsky listed the men arrested in the fourth week of December and charged with being the "Moscow Center" of the clandestine Zinovievist organization whose Leningrad Center had carried out Kirov's murder. Trotsky wrote:

> ... these fifteen individuals are implicated, no more, no less, in the assassination of Kirov and, according to explanations given by Pravda, **they had as their aim the seizure of power, beginning with Leningrad, "with the secret intention of reestablishing the capitalist régime."**

Trotsky thought that this charge was important enough to devote two paragraphs to denouncing it:

3. Was the Purpose to Restore Capitalism?

> The first question which must inevitably arise in the minds of all thinking workers is the following: How could it come to pass that at a time like this, after all the economic successes, after the "abolition" – according to official assurances – of classes in the USSR, and the "construction" of the socialist society – **how could it come to pass that old Bolsheviks, the most intimate collaborators of Lenin, those who shared power with Stalin, members of the "Old Guard," could have posed for their task the restoration of capitalism?** Do Zinoviev, Kamenev and the others consider that the socialist régime is no boon to the masses? Or, on the contrary, do

they expect from capitalism personal advantages both for themselves and their descendants? And what sort of advantages?

Only utter imbeciles would be capable of thinking that capitalist relations, that is to say, the private ownership of the means of production, including the land, can be reestablished in the USSR by peaceful methods and lead to the régime of bourgeois democracy. As a matter of fact, even if it were possible in general, capitalism could not be regenerated in Russia except as the result of a savage counter-revolutionary coup d'état which would cost ten times as many victims as the October Revolution and the civil war. In the event of the overthrow of the Soviets, their place could only be taken by a distinctly Russian Fascism, so ferocious that in comparison to it the ferocity of the Mussolini régime and that of Hitler would appear like philanthropic institutions. Zinoviev and Kamenev are no fools. They cannot but understand that the restoration of capitalism would first of all sig-nify the total extermination of the revolutionary genera-tion, themselves, of course, included. Consequently, there cannot be the slightest doubt here that **the accu-sation concocted by Stalin against the Zinoviev** group is fraudulent from top to bottom, both as regards the goal specified – restoration of capitalism; and as regards the means – terrorist acts.

Trotsky repeated this accusation in an article dated January 26, 1935, published in the February 1935 issue number 42 of the B.O.:

The first government communique and official articles after the arrest of the Moscow group of Old Bolsheviks said that Zinoviev-Kamenev and their friends had taken as their aim "**the restoration of the capitalist system**" and they were trying to provoke "armed intervention" from abroad (by the intermediacy of a consul- from Lat-via!). No serious person could believe it; that is under-stood.

Stalin's lackeys, who cover themselves with the name of "leaders" of the Communist International, don't, however, recoil at the assertion that Zinoviev, Kamenev and the others "have themselves admitted their crimes." Which ones? Preparation of **the restoration of capitalism**? Preparation of armed intervention?

...

Let us admit that Zinoviev's criticism was false. Let us even grant that the lackeys were right to judge criticism directed against them "criminal. " But are we to see in that the "**restoration of capitalism**" and "armed intervention"? What connection is there between the demand for a more revolutionary policy against the bourgeoisie and a program for "the restoration of a bourgeois regime"? Where has common sense gone? It is completely buried beneath a monstrous defecation of infamy.[1]

Trotsky continued to repeat this charge in B.O. #43, of April 1935:

Today Maisky, in the rank of ambassador, accuses "Zinovievists" and "Trotskyists" of striving to **provoke military intervention in order to restore capitalism**...[2]

...

In the government communiqué as well as in numerous articles in *Pravda* there was, as is well known, the direct and categorical assertion that Zinoviev and Kamenev

---

[1] Trotsky, "Everything Gradually Falls Into Place." WLT 1934-1935 223-228. Originally in B.O. #42.
[2] "The Workers' State, Thermidor and Bonapartism." WLT 1934-1935 240-261, at 251. Originally in B.O. #43.

had as their goal the restoration of capitalism and military intervention...[3]

And in B.O. #44 of July 1935:

Of the six congresses in the history of the Comintern to date, **Zinoviev** was president of five. Now he is in prison, ostensibly for **having wanted to restore capitalism** by a terrorist act...[4]

Trotsky and his son Leon Sedov repeated this charge yet again in their attack on the August 1936 Moscow Trial of Zinoviev, Kamenev, and others in B.O. #52-53, republished in French as Leon Sedov, *Livre rouge sur le procès de Moscou / Red Book on the Moscow Trial* (October 1937).

16-го января 1935 года в советских газетах появился обвинительный акт по делу, так называемого, Московского центра, с Зиновьевым, Каменевым, Евдокимовым и др. во главе.... 15-16 января состоялся суд над Зиновьевым, Каменевым и др. всего 19 подсудимыми. **Они обвинялись в стремлении к "реставрации капитализма"** и в контр-революционной деятельности вообще. Ни одного конкретного факта или доказательства обвинение не привело. (В.О. #52)

In *Le livre rouge*:

Le 16 janvier 1935, les journaux soviétiques publiaient l'acte d'accusation de l 'affaire du prétendu Centre de Moscou, avec Zinoviev, Kaménev, Evdokimov et autres en tête. ... Les 15 et 16 janvier, le tribunal statuait sur le sort de Zinoviev, de Kamenev, etc., 19 inculpés en tout.

---

[3] "Notes of a Journalist." WLT 1934-1935 323-238, at 327. Originally in B.O. #43. Italics in original, boldface mine, GF.

[4] "The Seventh Congress of the Comintern." (June 7, 1935). WLT 1934-1935,406-406, at 405. Originally in B.O. #44.

> **Ils étaient accusés d'aspirer au «rétablissement du capitalisme»** et de mener une activité contrerévolutionnaire *en général*. Aucun fait concret, aucune preuve ne furent apportés par accusation. (*Livre rouge*, pp. 23-24)

In *The Red Book*:

> On January 16, 1935, the Soviet newspapers published the formal indictment in the case of the so-called Moscow Center, with Zinoviev, Kamenev, Evdokimov and the others at its head. ... On January 15 and 16 the court pronounced judgment on the fate of Zinoviev, Kamenev, et al., 19 defendants in all. **They were accused of striving for the "restoration of capitalism"** and of counter-revolutionary activity in general. Not a single concrete fact, no proof, was introduced by the prosecution.[5]

This charge is again repeated in the following section (called "chapters" in the French and English books):

> **"Реставрация капитализма"** или "жажда личной власти"?

> В связи с первым процессом, Зиновьева и Каменева обвинили в том, что они за возврат к капитализму, "за капиталистическую реставрацию." Под этим припевом шла в советских газетах того времени (начало 1935 года) травля Зиновьева -- Каменева.

> Если не удалось – тогда – установить характера деятельности Зиновьева -- Каменева (террор), **то по**

---

[5] Leon Sedov, *The Red Book on the Moscow Trials* (1936), Chapter 3. At http://www.marxists.org/history/etol/writers/sedov/works/red/ch03.htm (Red Book)

крайней мере твердо была установлена их цель: восстановление капитализма.

На втором процессе "капиталистическая реставрация" была совершенно забыта. Дана была новая версия: ...«с несомненностью установлено, что единственным мотивом организации троцкистско-зиновьевского блока явилось стремление во что бы то ни стало захватить власть» (обвинительный акт). (В.О. #52)

From the Livre rouge:

Le «rétablissement du capitalisme» ou la «soif du pouvoir personnel»?

En liaison avec le premier procès, Zinoviev et Kaménev avaient été accusés d'être pour le retour au capitalism, pour la *«restauration capitaliste»*. C'est avec ce refrain que les journaux soviétiques de l'époque (début 1935) ont poursuivi Zinoviev et Kaménev.

Si l'on ne pouvait alors etablir le caractère de l'activité de Zinoviev et de Kaménev (la terreur), on avait du moins nettement établi leur but: *le rétablissement du capitalisme.*

Au second procès, le «rétablissement du capitalisme» est tout a fait oublié. On apporte une nouvelle version: " ... Il est établi d'une façon irréfutable que le seul motif de l'organisation du bloc trotskiste-zinoviéviste fut la tendance à s'emparer coûte que coûte du pouvoir" (1). (*Livre rouge*, p. 34)

From *The Red Book*:

The "Restoration of Capitalism" or the "Thirst for Personal Power"?

In connection with the first trial[6], Zinoviev and Kamenev had been accused of supporting the return to capitalism, "capitalist restoration." It is with this refrain that the Soviet newspapers of that period (the beginning of 1935) persecuted Zinoviev and Kamenev.

If one could not – then – establish the nature of the activity of Zinoviev and Kamenev (terror), **at least their purpose had been clearly established: the re-establishment of capitalism.**

At the second trial, the "restoration of capitalism" was completely forgotten. A new version was given: "... It is irrefutably established that the only motive for the organization of the Trotskyist-Zinovievist block was the attempt to seize power at any cost." (The Indictment). (Red Book, Chapter 4)

Trotsky continued to repeat this charge long after the First Moscow Trial of August 1936. In the middle of his lengthy final statement at the Dewey Commission hearings in April, 1937 – a statement that occupies 171 pages of print in the published transcript, *The Case of Leon Trotsky* – Trotsky made the following statement:

In January, 1935 Zinoviev, Kamenev, and others were sentenced, in connection with the Kirov assassination, to some years of imprisonment. **During the trial they confessed a desire "to restore capitalism."** (533.)[7]

In another undated article of about this time Trotsky again repeats the same charge:

---

[6] Trotsky is referring to the Moscow Center trial of January 1935.
[7] Commission of inquiry into the charges made against Leon Trotsky in the Moscow trials. Preliminary Commission Coyoacán, Mexico, 1937. *The Case of Leon Trotsky. Report of hearings on the charges made against him in the Moscow trials. By the Preliminary Commission of Inquiry: John Dewey, chairman [and others].* New York: Harper & Brothers, 1937. (CLT)

These questions relate above all to Zinoviev and Kamenev. Just what were their motives – and these motives must have been exceptionally forceful – that guided them in their purported terror? **At the first trial in January 1935**, Zinoviev and Kamenev, while denying their participation in the assassination of Kirov, did acknowledge, by way of compensation, their "moral responsibility" for the terrorist tendencies, and in doing so **they cited** as the incentive for their oppositional activity **their urge "to restore capitalism."** If we had nothing else to go by except this inhuman political "confession," it would be sufficient to expose the lie of Stalinist justice.[8]

Trotsky's "Amalgam"

All these statements of Trotsky's are false. No such charge or anything like it figures in either the December 28, 1934, indictment of the Leningrad Zinovievist group charged with the assassination of Sergei Kirov or the January 1935 trial indictment (*obvinitel'noe zakliuchenie*) published in *Pravda*, January 16, 1935, on page 6. Nothing at all about restoring capitalism, or even the word "capitalism" itself, can be found among the charges as listed in the "rehabilitation" document published in the official Gorbachev-era Party journal *Izvestia Tsentral'nogo Komiteta KPSS* in 1989.[9] Even the archival copy of the court's sentence against the defendants in this case fails to mention anything about reestablishing capitalism.[10] Indeed, the word "capitalism" does not occur in any of these documents at all.[11]

---

[8] Trotsky, "Zinoviev And Kamenev" (1937). At
http://www.marxists.org/archive/trotsky/1937/xx/kamzinov.htm
[9] "O dele tak nazivaemogo «moskovskogo tsentra,"" *Izvestia TsK KPSS* 7 (1989), p. 65. Reprinted in book form in R-PP 149.
[10] Volkogonov Papers (LOC) Reel 3 Container 4 Folder 16.
[11] Trotsky does not identify the passage from *Pravda* where he supposedly found the phrase "with the secret intention of reestablishing the capitalist régime." I have not been able to find it anywhere in the December 1934 pages of that

The transcript of this January 1935 trial has never been published, so I have not seen it, and Trotsky did not read it either. However, some quotations from the words of a few of the defendants were reproduced in a newspaper article which I discuss below. Trotsky quoted from it in 1936, as we shall see. But in it none of the accused confessed to desiring "to restore capitalism."

The passage from Chapter 3 of the *Red Book* quoted above correctly identifies the date, January 16, 1935, that the indictment (*obvinitel'nyi akt*) against Zinoviev, Kamenev, and their Moscow-based supporters was published in Soviet newspapers, including *Pravda.* But nothing about this charge or anything like it can be found there.

There is no question about the use of different texts. In the paragraphs immediately before the section subtitled "The 'Restoration of Capitalism' or the 'Thirst for Personal Power'" (quoted above) Trotsky/Sedov quote from the statements of four of the January 1935 defendants: Kamenev, Bakaev, Zinoviev, and Evdokimov. The quotations from the first three are taken directly from the text of the indictment which, as Trotsky/Sedov correctly noted, was published in *Pravda* and other Soviet newspapers on January 16, 1935 (in *Pravda* on page 6).

> 18. Каменев Л.Б ... Признал, что «недостаточно активно и энергично боролся с тем разложением, которое было последствием борьбы с партией и на почве которого могла возникнуть и осуществить своё преступление шайка бандитов из подонков антипартийной оппозиции.»

Translated:

---

newspaper. Of course, even if it should be found there somewhere it would not change matters.

This, by the way, is a legitimate example of "absence of evidence" constituting "evidence of absence, " because *Pravda* of December 1934 to January 1935 is a finite search field.

Kamenev acknowledged that he "did not fight actively or energetically enough against the demoralization which was the consequence of the struggle against the party and upon which ground a band of brigands (Nikolaev and others) could spring up and carry out their crime."

... не порвал окончательно с Зиновьевым своих связей ... (col. 3)

Translated:

"[acknowledged] ... that he did not break all ties with Zinoviev."

Здесь была только злобная враждебная критика важнейших мероприятий партии ... (col. 1, bottom)

Translated:

[Bakaev declares that] "here [among the Zinovievists] there was only malevolent and hostile criticism of the most important measures taken by the party."

... партия совершщенно права в том, что она говорит по вопросу о политической ответственности бывшей антипартийной «зиновьевской» группы за совершившееся убийство. (col. 3)

Translated:

[Zinoviev says that] " ... the party is absolutely correct when it speaks of the political responsibility of the old 'Zinovievist' anti-party group for the assassination which has just been accomplished."[12]

The quotation from Evdokimov is taken directly from the separate article published on the same page opposite the text of the indictment and titled "From the Hall of the Supreme Court of the USSR.

---

[12] See *Livre rouge*, 33.

Declaration of the defendant Evdokimov to the court of January 15 of this year."[13]

> «... · мы должны нести ответственности, ибо тот яд, которым мы отравили окружающим нас в течение десятка лет, способствовал совершению преступления – убийству Кирова.» (col. 6, top)

Translated:

> "We must bear the responsibility [for Kirov's murder], because it is the venom with which we poisoned those around us during a 10-year period which made possible the realization of this crime." [14]

The article quoting Evdokimov is summarized in *Humanité* of January 18, 1935.[15] Trotsky and Sedov had read either the Russian original in *Pravda* or the briefer French summary. In *Pravda*, the Evdokimov article and the text of the Indictment are on the same page.

Therefore Trotsky and Sedov knew that Zinoviev, Kamenev and the other defendants, arrested in December 1934 and put on trial in mid-January 1935, were not charged with conspiring to "restore capitalism" or "provoking armed intervention." They did not confess to it, nor did the issue arise in any way.

Rogovin's "Amalgam"

Vadim Z. Rogovin was a historian whose works constitute the most sustained Trotskyist interpretation of Soviet history of the Stalin

---

[13] "Iz zala verkhovnogo suda SSSR. Zaiavlenie podsudimogo Evdokimova na sude 15 ianvaria sego goda." *Pravda* January 16, 1935, page 6, cols 5-6.
[14] See *Livre rouge*, 34.
[15] "Les contre-révolutionnaires devant le tribunal supreme." *Humanité* January 18, 1935, p. 3 cols. 6-7. More quotations from Evdokimov are translated in an article the following day: "'Ennemis dangereux le Tribunal les met sous les verrous,' écrivent les 'Izvestia.'" *Humanité* Jan. 19, 1935, p. 2 col. 1.

period. In his books, Rogovin always cited Trotsky prominently and positively. But Rogovin could not find any evidence of the "restoration of capitalism" charge that Trotsky claimed was in newspaper accounts. Rather than acknowledge this fact, however, Rogovin just repeated Trotsky's claim without any footnote or citation.

> In the newspaper commentaries accompanying the trial transcript, the desire to restore capitalist society in the USSR was given as the incentive for these terrorist moods and for oppositional inclinations in general.[16]

Rogovin realized that the "restoration of capitalism" charge was not mentioned in the August 1936 trial. But instead of noting the fact that Trotsky (and Sedov) lied about this, Rogovin himself concocted a lie. We may call "Rogovin's amalgam" — a story according to which Zinoviev and Kamenev made a deal with Stalin to withdraw this charge, in return for which they would plead guilty to terrorist activity. Rogovin cites no evidence for such a deal, and we have none today. Rogovin then refers to "the shift from the version about wanting to restore capitalism to the one about the naked thirst for power" (28).

In this way, Rogovin avoided exposing Trotsky's lie through a lie of his own. Perhaps he believed he was saving Trotsky's reputation. After all, how many people would scour the Soviet press to see whether the "restoration of capitalism" charge was actually raised in it?

Even nineteen months later, at the First Moscow Trial of August 1936, this charge was not part of the indictment, or charges against the defendants, including Zinoviev and Kamenev. In fact, nothing about the "restoration of capitalism" was mentioned in any way during that trial. Zinoviev, Kamenev, et al. did *not* confess to anything even remotely resembling this. They were *not* charged

---

[16] Rogovin, *1937. Stalin's Year of Terror*. Oak Park, IL: Mehring Books, 1998, p. 26.

with supporting any "return to capitalism," "restoration of capitalism," etc.

This charge is a fabrication by Trotsky. Once again, to use Trotsky's own term, this story is an "amalgam." It is not true that, as
Trotsky/Sedov claimed, "'the restoration of capitalism' was completely forgotten" at the First Moscow Trial of August 1936. There
was nothing to "forget." This accusation had never been made in
the first place.

Why Did Trotsky Lie About This?

Pierre Broué and Vadim Rogovin wrote that Trotsky and Sedov
lied about the bloc with the Zinovievists, Rights, and other oppositionists, and about Trotsky's contacts with some of the other people with whom he publicly and repeatedly denied having had any
contact, because they did not want to endanger supporters in the
Soviet Union whom the NKVD had not yet identified. In a previous
chapter I have argued this cannot be the correct explanation.

Moreover, this explanation does not apply to Trotsky's claim that
Zinoviev, Kamenev, et al. were accused of, and confessed to, plotting to restore capitalism. Anyone who bothered to obtain and
read the issues of *Pravda* could have discovered that Trotsky was
lying. Therefore, Trotsky had to know that by making this claim he
was taking a serious risk of being exposed as a liar.

Once again, Trotsky must have had some very compelling reason
for taking such a risk. A statement attributed to psychoanalyst Al-
fred Adler runs: "A lie would have no sense unless the truth were
felt to be dangerous." Trotsky would not have lied if the truth had
been on his side. It follows that he was hiding something. What
dangerous truth was Trotsky concealing?

"Expose the Scheme In Advance"

Towards the end of his December 30, 1934, article on the Kirov
Assassination Trotsky inserted a section titled "The Inevitability of

New Amalgams Had Been Foretold." In it, he claimed to have "predicted" that his own name would soon be raised "alongside Zinoviev's."

> When the first dispatch appeared in which Nikolaiev was said to have been a member of the Leningrad Opposition in 1926, there was no further room for doubt. The new campaign against Zinoviev and Kamenev was not long in following. At that moment, in a conversation with a friend (I apologize for these personal details, but they are necessary for the understanding of the psychological undercurrents in the case), I said, "The matter will not rest long on this plane. Tomorrow they will bring Trotskyism to the fore." To be able to make such a prediction, it was really not necessary to be a prophet. The December 25 issue of the *Temps* which I received two or three days later contained in a telegraphic dispatch from Moscow the following item: "We must point out ... that as the days go by, Trotsky's name is being mentioned more and more often alongside Zinoviev's." Kirov's corpse and the Zinoviev group thus become preparatory steps for a much wider and bolder scheme: to deal a blow at international Leninism.[17]

We know now how Trotsky was able to "predict" this. In 1980, Pierre Broué found proof in the newly-opened Harvard Trotsky Archive that Trotsky and his Soviet-based followers really were in a bloc with the Zinovievists. Once the Zinovievists had inculpated their own leaders by name there was no reason for them not to also name Trotsky. Therefore it was "predictable" that they would do so.

Trotsky chose not to reveal that he and his followers in the USSR were in a bloc with the Zinovievists, the Rights, and some other oppositionists. That meant he had to account for the progressive

---

[17] "The Stalinist Bureaucracy and the Kirov assassination." December 28, 1934. WLT 1934-1935 175-197, at 194.

revelations by the NKVD and Soviet prosecution in some other way.

So he created an "amalgam." According to this false story, the "campaign" against the Zinovievists was a "preparatory step" to "a much wider and bolder scheme": namely, an attack on Trotsky himself and his new movement. Trotsky claimed that his name was brought up because of Soviet alarm at "the growth of international Leninism," as he called the Trotskyist movement.

Of course, Trotsky knew better. Since Broué's 1980 article, we have known better too.

Then Trotsky wrote:

> There is only one way to forestall en route the amalgams that are in preparation: *Expose the scheme in advance.* The Stalinists are trying to mold the public opinion of the world police towards expulsions, extraditions, arrests and other more decisive measures. The Leninists must prepare the public opinion of the world proletariat for these possible events. (195; italics in the original.)

Here, Trotsky explicitly claims that he "predicted" his name would come up so that he could "forestall" future fabrications – show them to be false because "predictable." In reality, the truth appears to be that Trotsky was able to "predict" things that he knew would come to light because they were true.

Hypothesis

This suggests an explanation for Trotsky's claim that Zinoviev, Kamenev, and the rest were charged "with the secret intention of reestablishing the capitalist régime," and his persistence in repeating it over and over again. Our hypothesis is that he did so because the charge was true – not only about Zinoviev and Kamenev but, more importantly, about Trotsky himself. According to testimony in the 1937 and 1938 Moscow Trials, Trotsky really had instructed his followers that re-establishing capitalism would be necessary in order to placate the Germans and Japanese.

Trotsky may have been prompted to anticipate this charge by a press release printed in *Humanité* of December 23, 1934 (p. 5 col. 7) which states that the restoration of capitalism was the goal of the Kirov assassins, the Leningrad Center: "la préoccupation secrète de restaurer le régime capitaliste." This accusation is *not* leveled at Zinoviev, Kamenev, et al., whose arrests are signaled in a brief article immediately below the former.

An article in *Humanité* the following day (Dec. 24, p.3) titled "Le groupe terroriste zinovévist-trotskiste est le résultat de la persistence dans l'opposition à la ligne du parti" quotes *Izvestia* of December 22 or 23 as follows:

> Le sens entier de leur activité et de leurs aspirations était la restauration du régime capitaliste.

Translated:

> The whole sense of their activity and hopes was the restoration of the capitalist regime.

This too is stated of the Kirov assassins, not of Zinoviev and Kamenev. Trotsky cited *Humanité* as a source for his early article on the Kirov murder.

These articles concern only the Leningrad-based Zinovievists who were charged with murdering Kirov. Moreover, it only claims that the "sense" of their program would be a reversion to capitalist forms of production and distribution characteristic of the New Economic Policy – which, of course, they were.[18] There is no indication in this article or any other that Zinoviev, Kamenev, and the

---

[18] The *Humanité* article makes it clear that the Soviets knew that the economic programs of the Zinovievists was close to that of Trotsky. Trotsky's 1929 economic critique of the collectivization-industrialization campaign and that of the Right's Riutin Program of 1932 are similar, and Trotsky's came first.

Moscow-based Zinovievists, under arrest by December 22, were to be charged with plotting to restore capitalism.

Trotsky must have assumed this charge would be brought forth quickly, just as he assumed his name would be mentioned very soon. In the latter case, he was correct – Trotsky's name came up almost immediately. In the former case, though, Trotsky miscalculated. In 1935, Zinoviev and Kamenev did not expose the bloc and the "parallel," or secret, leadership. The charge of "plotting to restore capitalism" was not brought up against Trotsky until sometime after the First Moscow Trial of August 1936.

However, Trotsky could reasonably have anticipated that this charge against him might be still brought up at some future time. Once Zinoviev and Kamenev had been arrested it was possible that they would name Radek, Piatakov, and Sokol'nikov. But Trotsky could not have known in advance when this might happen or when the charge against him would be made public.

If this was Trotsky's plan it made a good deal of sense. If the names of the leaders of the "parallel center" Radek, Piatakov, and Sokol'nikov did not come up or if, when interrogated, these men did not reveal Trotsky's plans, Trotsky could simply continue to claim that Stalin had made the "restoration of capitalism" charge and then abandoned it. Trotsky could then cite this as further "proof" of Stalin's duplicity. In fact, Trotsky and Sedov did make this claim, as we have seen:

> At the second trial, the "restoration of capitalism" was completely forgotten.

But if, as eventually did happen, the charge of plotting "the restoration of capitalism" was raised against him Trotsky would have the option of claiming that he had once again refuted an "amalgam in preparation" by "exposing the scheme in advance." So Trotsky continued to repeat the baseless charge that Zinoviev and Kamenev had been accused of plotting to "restore capitalism."

According to this hypothesis, therefore, Trotsky was able to make this assumption with some confidence *because he had indeed instructed his followers in exactly this way – to restore capitalism.* Trotsky's repeated claim in December-January 1934-5 that the Soviet government had charged Zinoviev, Kamenev, et al. with plotting to "reestablish the capitalist regime" can be explained as Trotsky's attempt to anticipate accusations that he assumed would probably be made against himself sometime in the future.

Under this hypothesis Trotsky's "prediction" that the defendants would be charged with reestablishing capitalism is like his "prediction" that his own name would soon be raised in the Kirov assassination case. In both instances Trotsky knew the charge against him was true and would almost certainly be made sooner or later. By anticipating this charge – by "exposing the scheme in advance" – Trotsky hoped to prepare public opinion – or, at any rate, his own supporters, the people who read his Bulletin – for the time when the Soviets really did make it, and so to "refute" it in advance by making it look all too "predictable" and therefore false.

Radek's and Piatakov's Testimony

This accusation that Trotsky was overtly proposing the "restoration of capitalism" did finally surface during the Second Moscow Trial in January 1937. It was a major, and shocking, feature of the trial. Trotsky, widely considered a fiery revolutionary more "left" than Stalin, was accused of promoting the re-establishment of capitalism, or at least many aspects of it, since that seemed to be the only way to get the help of the capitalist powers to overthrow Stalin.

Iurii Piatakov, one of the chief defendants (the trial is often called "the Radek-Piatakov trial") testified:

> As for the **retreat**, Trotsky wrote that Radek and I were mistaken in thinking that the **retreat** would be inconsiderable -- we would have to **retreat** very far, and on this was based the bloc, not only with the Zinovievites, but also with the Rights. (1937 Trial 38-39)

... In this connection also it would be necessary, for considerations of home policy, to effect a fairly big **retreat**,
in addition to concessions to foreigners. Radek quite
justly mentioned this **retreat** in town and country, such
as permitting capitalist trade and so forth. To put it simply, Trotsky explained that it would be a very serious **retreat**. This is exactly what he said: you and Radek are
still under the sway of the old ideas of 1925-26 and you
are unable to see that in essence our coming to power
will mean that we will have to **retreat very far in the
direction of capitalism.** (1937 Trial 65)

Karl Radek outlined how Trotsky's views changed between 1934
and 1935:

VYSHINSKY: Three facts: the April letter of 1934, the December letter of 1935 and Piatakov's meeting with Trotsky in December 1935. How was the question put in
Trotsky's letter in 1934? War, working for defeat?

RADEK: Yes.

VYSHINSKY: A return to capitalism in substance?

RADEK: No, a return to capitalism is not raised in the letter.

VYSHINSKY: No? What then?

RADEK: A **retreat** which we then thought. . . .

VYSHINSKY: To where?

RADEK: To the positions of the NEP, with industry
strengthened in comparison with what it had been before 1928.

VYSHINSKY: A **retreat** towards strengthening what elements?

RADEK: A **retreat** which was to restore a part of the capitalist elements as well, but this **retreat**, if compared with the state of things in 1927 – there would be a possibility during this **retreat**, on the one hand, of admitting capitalist restoration, but at the same time of strengthening industry, thanks to the First Five-Year Plan, the state farms and part of the collective farms – that is to say, we would have an economic base on which in my opinion a proletarian government could have maintained itself.

VYSHINSKY: So a proletarian government could still have maintained itself? But the tendency was to go backward?

RADEK: The tendency was to go backward.

VYSHINSKY: In 1935 this stood out more clearly in comparison with 1934?

RADEK: In 1935 the question was raised **of going back to capitalism.**

VYSHINSKY: To what limits?

RADEK: What Trotsky proposed was without any limits. To such limits as the enemy might require. (122)

According to Sokol'nikov the Trotskyists understood that they had no choice; it was retreat or be crushed:

SOKOLNIKOV: ... We considered that fascism was the most organized form of capitalism, that it would triumph, would seize Europe and stifle us. It was therefore better to come to terms with it, it was better to consent to a compromise in the sense of **retreating from socialism to capitalism.** (151)

The hypothesis that Trotsky did advocate the "restoration of capitalism" as Radek, Piatakov, and others asserted, is consistent with much other evidence we now possess.

Radek, Piatakov and Sokol'nikov also testified that Trotsky was
directly conspiring with the Germans and Japanese. Such negotia-
tion is a logical corollary to the assumption that the USSR would be
defeated in a war and the Stalin leadership overthrown. The Germans and Japanese would have to be persuaded to allow the opposition to take power rather than simply to dismember the USSR by
themselves. Trotsky allegedly either assumed or knew for a fact
that Germany and Japan would demand considerable territorial
concessions – the Ukraine and the Pacific Coast region – as well as
economic concessions, as their price.

Thanks to the partial opening of some former Soviet archives, we
possess a great deal of Soviet evidence to corroborate the Moscow
Trial testimony that Trotsky was conspiring with the Germans and
Japanese. There is no indication that this evidence was faked.
Moreover, there appears to be no reason to suspect it was faked
since it was all secret until the partial opening of Soviet archives
after the end of the USSR.[19] This evidence is consistent with the
testimony that Trotsky was planning to "restore capitalism" in the
sense of making serious economic (as well as territorial) concessions to the fascist powers.

Trotsky's 1930 Program

The program of "restoring capitalism" that, according to Radek
and Piatakov, Trotsky outlined to them, is closely similar to what
Trotsky had openly advocated when the collectivization-
industrialization campaign was under way. Here are some of Trotsky's programmatic proposals from issue #10 of the *Bulletin of the
Russian Opposition* [20] dated March 23, 1930, in the article titled

---

[19] We examine this evidence in *Leon Trotsky's Collaboration with Germany and
Japan*, and will examine yet more evidence in a subsequent book to be published
in 2020.
[20] This is the title Trotsky used in translation. In Russian it is just "Bulletin of the
Opposition."

"Open Letter to the Communist Party of the Soviet Union. The State of the Party and the Tasks of the Left Opposition":

> A **retreat** is inevitable in any case. It must be carried out as soon as possible and as orderly as possible.
>
> Put an end to "complete" collectivization, replacing it with a careful selection based on a real freedom of choice ... Put an end to the policy of administrative abolition of the kulak. Curbing the exploiting tendencies of the kulak will remain a necessary policy for many years.
>
> Put an end to the "racetrack-gallop" pace of industrialization. Re-evaluate the question of the tempos of development in the light of experience, taking into account the necessity of raising the standard of living of the masses. Pose point-blank the question of the quality of production, as vital for the consumer as it is for the producer.
>
> Give up the "ideal" of a closed economy. Work out a new variant of the plans based on as much interaction as possible with the world market.
>
> To make the necessary **retreat**, to renew its [the USSR's] strategic arsenal without too much damage and without losing its sense of perspective ...[21]

The abandonment of collectivization, of the destruction of the kulaks as a class, and of crash industrialization, a greatly increased role for foreign trade, and what Trotsky termed the "necessity" of raising the standard of living – these policies (if they were possible at all) would have meant a greater reliance on markets and a smaller role for the state. Trotsky was advocating a form of state-regulated capitalist commodity production similar to that of the New Economic Policy. Trotsky justified this as an "inevitable" and a "necessary retreat."

---

[21] WLT 1930 135-150, at 147, 150.

This 1929 program of Trotsky's is similar to the Rights' "Riutin Platform" of 1932.[22] Arch Getty noted that Trotsky's program in the 1930s was not essentially different from that of the Rights.

> ... Trotsky's spirited defence of the *smychka* and rural market relations, his criticism of the ultra-leftist campaign against the kulaks, and his advocacy of planning on the basis of "real potentials" were similar to the strictures of Bukharin's "Notes of an Economist." (Getty TIE 34 note 21)

> Although the Riutin Platform originated in the right wing of the Bolshevik Party, its specific criticisms of the Stalinist regime were in the early 1930s shared by the more leftist Leon Trotsky, ... Like the Riutin group, Trotsky believed that the Soviet Union in 1932 was in a period of extreme crisis provoked by Stalin's policies. Like them, he believed that the rapid pace of forced collectivization was a disaster and that the hurried and voluntarist nature of industrial policy made rational planning impossible, resulting in a disastrous series of economic "imbalances." Along with the Riutinists, Trotsky called for a drastic change in economic course and democratization of the dictatorial regime within a party that suppressed all dissent. According to Trotsky, Stalin had brought the country to ruin.[23]

The economic section[24] of the "Riutin Platform" shows clear similarities to Trotsky's proposals:

----

[22] We now know this was composed not by Riutin but by Bukharin, Tomsky, and other leaders of the Rights. See also Furr, Stalin Waiting, Chapter 8, "The 'Riutin Platform' Was Really the 'Bukharin Platform.'"
[23] Getty and Naumov Road 61.
[24] The full title of the document known as the "Riutin Platform" is "Stalin and the Crisis of the Proletarian Dictatorship. Platform of the 'Union of Marxist-Leninists' (the 'Riutin Group')." It was first published in R-PP 334-443. There is now an

III. In the field of industrialization.

1. The immediate cessation of anti-Leninist methods of industrialization and growth in the game of pace by robbing the working class, civil servants and village through direct and indirect, overt and concealed unbearable taxes and inflation. Industrialization on the basis of the actual and the steady growth of the welfare of the masses.

2. Reduction of investment in capital construction in accordance with the general condition of all the available resources of the country.

IV. In the field of agriculture.

1. Immediate dissolution of all the inflated collective farms (kolkhozy) formed by force. Truly voluntary collectivization on the basis of machine technology and all possible assistance to collective farms.

2. Immediate creation of all necessary conditions and real support for the development of individual poor and middle peasant farming.

3. Elimination of all unprofitable collective farms. Retention in our hands only of that number of the best collective farms that we are actually able to make truly exemplary socialist enterprises.

4. Transmission of large-scale machine inventory of liquidated state and collective farms into the hands of local agricultural machinery associations.

English translation: Sobhanlal Datta Gupta, ed. The Ryutin Platform. Stalin and the Crisis of Proletarian Dictatorship. Platform of the "Union of Marxists-Leninists." Translated by Pranab Ghosh and Susmita Bhattacharya. Kolkata: Seribaan, 2010. The economic section of the Riutin Platform is extremely skimpy. It takes up fewer than two pages in a document 112 pages long in the printed edition.

...

6. The immediate cessation of grain, and harvesting seizure campaigns and seizures of other agricultural products, [which are] modern methods of robbing the village.

Land development and consolidation of individual farm-
ers and confirming their long-term use of the allocated
land.

V. In the area of trade.

1. Cessation of exports of agricultural products at very
low prices.

2. Cessation of exports of consumer goods at very low
prices.

3. Return to the Leninist policy of prices. A decisive de-
cline in prices. Restoration of cooperation and its rights.

VI. In the field of finance and tax.

I. The termination of inflation, heavy tax burden on the
proletariat and all workers.

2. Termination of the endless exactions of every kind in
the form of loans placed by virtually mandatory continuing increase in pay differentials in cooperation, etc.

3. A maximum and effective reduction of taxes on workers, employees and workers of the village.

VII. In the field of legal material living conditions of
workers and peasants.

1. Restore all of the rights of workers to clothing, mar-
riage payment, etc., of which they have been deprived
during the past 4 years.

2. Restore the old rules of layoffs that existed 4 years ago.

3. Restore the old rules and a Leninist policy in the work of the trade unions.

4. Immediately stop the adventurist policy of dekulakization in the countryside, which is in fact aimed against the entire basic population of the village. (R-PP 441-3.)

The similarities between the Riutin Platform and Trotsky's "Open Letter" of 1930 are obvious. At the Second Moscow Trial in January 1937 Sokol'nikov stated:

As regards the principles of the program, as early as 1932 the Trotskyites, the Zinovievites, and the Rights had all come to agree in the main on the program which previously had been described as the program of the Rights.

This was the so-called Ryutin platform. As early as 1932 it expressed to a large extent just these principles of program which were common to all three groups. (1937 Trial 150-1)

The similarities between the "Riutin Platform" and Trotsky's proposals cannot be a coincidence. In 2004, an interrogation-confession of Valentin Astrov was published. Astrov was a student of Bukharin's and a member of his underground group of Rights. He revealed that the so-called "Riutin Platform" was not really written by Martemian Riutin at all, but by the leaders of the Rights, Rykov, Bukharin, Tomsky, and Uglanov.

Рютинская платформа по существу явилась документом не РЮТИНА, а центра правых... СЛЕПКОВ далее сообщил, что главными авторами рютинской платформы были РЫКОВ, БУХАРИН, ТОМСКИЙ и УГЛАНОВ и что было обусловлено в случае провала изобразить этот документ как документ только РЮТИНА, дабы не поставить под удар руководящую верхушку правых.

Translated:

> The Riutin Platform was in essence not RIUTIN'S document but that of the center of the Rights. ... SLEPKOV even stated that the main authors of the Riutin platform were RYKOV, BUKHARIN, TOMSKY, and UGLANOV and that it had been agreed, in the event of our failure [i.e. exposure, arrest] to depict this document as a document of RIUTIN alone, so as not to endanger the top leadership of the rights. (Lubianka 1937-1938 86.)

During the March 1938 Moscow Trial, Rykov confirmed what Astrov had stated in January 1937, that the Riutin Platform was composed by the leadership of the Rights: himself, Bukharin, Tomsky, Uglanov, and Vassilii Shmidt. Rykov also confirmed that it had been named after Riutin in order to provide cover for the leadership of the Rights.

> The platform was called after Ryutin, because it was published by supporters of the Rights, the Ryutin group, from Uglanov's Moscow organization. During the investigation instituted in connection with this platform, this group took the whole responsibility upon itself. This had been decided on beforehand, so that we ourselves should not be called to account for the platform... And to make it easier to do this, the program itself contained a phrase which expressed a certain sense of aloofness from Bukharin, Tomsky and myself; it said something to the effect that these three were waste steam. This was done from motives of double-dealing.

> (1938 Trial 163)

Bukharin confirmed what Astrov had testified:

> BUKHARIN: The Ryutin platform was adopted at the notorious conference held in the autumn of 1932, or in the summer, and it was approved at the meeting of which Alexei Ivanovich Rykov spoke.

VYSHINSKY: That means 1932?

BUKHARIN: The autumn of 1932. (1938 Trial 168)

Rykov's and Bukharin's testimony here is important to us since we know that Astrov was not subject to any kind of compulsion at his January 1937 interrogation. We also know that he testified truthfully because he had the chance to withdraw his testimony in 1989 and 1993, but instead he confirmed it. This constitutes further evidence that the confessions in the Moscow Trials are not fabrications forced upon innocent, unwilling defendants by the investigators or the prosecution but genuine confessions that represent what the defendants wished to say.[25]

Astrov testified that the Rights considered that the Trotskyists had adopted the economic program of the Rights:

> At the beginning of 1932 in a meeting of the activists of our organization in his apartment, SLEPKOV justified the necessity of concluding a bloc with the Trotskyists. He said that "the Trotskyists have accepted the economic platform of the Rights, and the Rights – the internal party program of the Trotskyists. The tactic of terror unites us. The disagreements between ourselves and the Trotskyists are insignificant." (32)

Bukharin confirmed this too in his testimony at the March 1938 trial:

> Much has been said here about the Ryutin platform, and perhaps there is no need to dwell upon it. It was called the Ryutin platform for reasons of secrecy, as an insurance against exposure; it was called the Ryutin platform in order to conceal the Right centre and its top leadership. Furthermore, I must say in addition: I think that the Ryutin platform—that is why I permit myself to hold

---

[25] I study this question in detail in the first section of *Trotsky's 'Amalgams'* and in *The Moscow Trials as Evidence*.

your attention for a few minutes longer—the Ryutin platform, as far as I can remember during the trial, **the platform of the Right counter revolutionary organization, was perhaps already actually a common platform of the other groupings, including the Kamenev-Zinoviev and Trotskyite groupings.**

It was just at this very moment that the situation became such that Trotsky had to throw off his Leftist uniform. When it came to exact formulations of what had to be done after all, his Right platform came into evidence at once, that is, he had to speak of decollectivization, etc.

VYSHINSKY: That is, you equipped Trotskyism ideologically too?

BUKHARIN: Quite true. (1938 Trial, 388-389)

Pierre Broué agreed that the Rights were part of the bloc.[26] Writing in 1980, Broué did not know that behind Riutin and Slepkov, whom he named, were Rykov, Bukharin, and Tomsky.

La lettre à l'encre sympathique de Léon Sedov fait apparaitre l'existence des groupes suivants : le groupe trotskyste d'U.R.S.S. (« notre fraction »), les « zinoviévistes ," le groupe d'I. N. Smirnov, le groupe Sten-Lominadzé, le groupe « Safar(ov)-Tarkhan(ov)," « les droitiers » et « les libéraux ." Bien entendu, tous ne participent pas au « bloc ," mais tous en connaissent l'existence et, selon Sedov, ont des contacts avec lui. (7)

Le groupe appelé par Sedov « les droitiers » pose en revanche plus de problèmes. Le terme désigne habituellement, on le sait, les éléments du parti qui ont, depuis l'époque de la Nep jusqu'à l'autocritique de leurs chefs de

---

[26] Broué, "Trotsky et le bloc des oppositions de 1932."CahLT 5 (Jan-Mar 1980), 7, 12, 14-16, 18,20, 28.

file, suivi le trio Boukharine, Rykov, Tomsky (26). ... les comptes rendus de réunions du secrétariat international de l'Opposition de gauche et quelques lettres de Léon Sedov font apparaître qu'il désigne systématiquement à l'époque par le terme de « droitiers » ce que les historiens désignent par « groupe Rioutine ," un groupe original apparu précisément en 1932. (12-13)

Translated:

The letter from Leon Sedov in invisible ink reveals the existence of the following groups: the Trotskyist group in the USSR ("our fraction"), the "Zinovievists," the group of I. N. Smirnov, the Sten-Lominadze group, the "Safar(ov)-Tarkhan(ov)" group, "the Rights" and "the liberals." Of course not all took part in the bloc but all of them knew of its existence and, according to Sedov, were in contact with him (7)

The group Sedov called "the Rights," by contrast, poses more problems. We know that the term usually means those elements of the Party who, since the NEP period until the self-criticisms of their leaders, had followed the troika of Bukharin, Rykov, and Tomsky (26). ... The accounts of the meetings of the international secretariat of the Left Opposition and a few letters from Leon Sedov reveal that at that time what the historians call the "Riutin group," an original group that appeared precisely in 1932, was systematically designated by the term "the Rights."

Broué goes on to name Galkin, Maretsky, Uglanov, and Kaiurov. The real history of the "Riutin group" was unknown to Broué, writing in 1980.

It is noteworthy that Broué recalls that Ante Ciliga, a dissident who was released and left the USSR, stated the relationship between the Rights and the Trotskyists in virtually the same words as Astrov:

> Ante Ciliga dit qu'il y affirmait : « Les droites ont eu rai-
> son dans le domaine économique et Trotsky dans la cri-
> tique du régime du parti (31). »[27]

Translated:

> Ante Ciliga said that said it was affirmed: "The Rights
> were correct in the economic arena, and Trotsky in the
> criticism of the regime of the Party."

Ciliga had this information at first hand, for he was imprisoned for
a time in the political "isolator" at Verkhneuralsk where a number
of Rights and Trotskyites, including both Astrov and I. N. Smirnov,
were also imprisoned and where the opposition conspiracy of the
bloc continued.[28]

Evidence and Proof

I have proposed the hypothesis that Trotsky did, in fact, advocate
as a "retreat" the restoration of many or most aspects of capitalism, as Radek, Piatakov, and Sokol'nikov testified at the January
1937 Moscow Trial. I believe this hypothesis is the only one that
can satisfy the following conditions:

* It explains why Trotsky again and again took the risk of exposure
as a liar by falsely claiming that Zinoviev and Kamenev had been
accused of, charged with, confessed to, and been convicted of

---

[27] Broué 14. Broué's reference is to A. Ciliga, *Au pays du grand mensonge*. Paris:
Gallimard, 1938. Published in English as *The Russian Enigma*. London: Ink Links
Ltd., 1979.
[28] "Arrested (in Russia) in 1930, he was imprisoned in the isolator at
Verkhneuralsk where he participated in the life of the 'Bolshevik-Leninist
collective' of which he offered a caricatural description after he was freed."
Stephen Schwartz, "Ante Ciliga (1898-1992): A Life at History's Crossroads."
Revolutionary History: Unpublished Articles, 34, at
https://web.archive.org/web/20010411013259/http://www.revolutionary-
history.co.uk/supplem.htm

"plotting to restore capitalism" and that this could be verified through articles in *Pravda*.

* It is consistent with the Riutin Platform of the Rights. We know that Trotsky approved the bloc with the Rights and other oppositionists in 1932, which was also the year that the Riutin Platform was adopted.

* It is consistent with the other evidence we now possess about the deliberate falsehoods Trotsky invented and repeated throughout the period under question. I examine them elsewhere in the present work.

* It is also consistent with the evidence we have collected from Soviet sources that Trotsky was indeed conspiring with Germany and Japan.[29]

* I have shown elsewhere[30] that Moscow Trials testimony is valid as evidence in that, whenever we can check it from independent sources, it turns out to reflect what the defendants chose to say rather than fabrications forced upon innocent defendants.

The defendants in the January 1937 Moscow Trial made it clear that Trotsky's plan to "retreat" to capitalism was motivated by his belief that the opposition could only come to power in one of two ways: either through a war with the fascist powers – which they assumed the USSR would lose – or through a *coup* against the Stalin leadership, which would only succeed in establishing itself with cooperation from other imperialist countries. In either case, German and Japanese cooperation would only be purchased at a very stiff price. According to them, Trotsky realized this and drew the necessary conclusions.

---

[29] See *Leon Trotsky's Collaboration with Germany and Japan*. I will publish much more evidence of Trotsky's collaboration in the next volume of studies of Trotsky during the 1930s.

[30] In the first part of Trotsky's 'Amalgams', and in The Moscow Trials as Evidence.

Considered dispassionately, the views these three defendants attributed to Trotsky make sense. Whether by assassination or by defeat in war at the hands of invaders, the removal by force of Stalin would certainly evoke a violent reaction, probably leading to rebellion and serious social instability. The Soviet Union's major capitalist enemies would likely try to take advantage of this situation, possibly by invading and attempting to dismember the enormous country and by setting up one or more capitalist regimes with political and social policies approved by them. To any Opposition that hoped to take the reins of power during such a crisis, it was obvious that some kind of agreement would have to be arranged, in advance, with these aggressive imperialist capitalist powers.

A Hypothesis Must Account for the Evidence

We have a lot of evidence, in the form of testimony at the 1937 and 1938 Moscow Trials, that Trotsky did advocate the "restoration of capitalism."

* His denial can be disregarded, because he would deny the charge whether he had advocated it or not, and because we know Trotsky lied when he thought it expedient.

*Trotsky's archive has been "purged," so the absence of evidence there of this or other conspiratorial aims can bear no weight.

Let us review the options:

1. That Trotsky did advocate "restoration of capitalism." This is the hypothesis that represents the most straightforward explanation in that it accounts for all the evidence.

2. That some other hypothesis can account for Trotsky's "amalgam" under consideration here: that Zinoviev and Kamenev were charged with, and confessed to, plotting "the restoration of capitalism."

This essay has laid out the evidence in support of hypothesis #1. As far as I can determine, there is no evidence to support *any* other hypothesis.

This leads us to an important conclusion. On the evidence, Trotsky did advocate the "restoration of capitalism" as Radek, Piatakov, and Sokol'nikov testified.

What does this mean for the further hypothesis that Trotsky conspired with Germany and Japan?

Evidence Internal to Trotsky's Writings

Trotsky was highly intelligent, a prolific writer, a skilled theorist, and a dedicated revolutionary activist. How then is it possible that Trotsky was an incompetent liar? Yet again and again he composed falsehoods that anyone could have discovered and exposed simply by checking the sources Trotsky himself cited.

But perhaps he wasn't an incompetent liar after all. Maybe he was intelligent enough to recognize that his acolytes were too devoted to check the veracity of his claims. His lies were "hidden in plain sight," as it were. Even so, it's taken a long while to uncover them. That would not speak to his incompetence as a liar—quite the opposite, really. All things considered, his career as a brazen phony was a great success!

The "restoration of capitalism" claim is one of these lies. During the period from December-January 1935 to January 1937 Trotsky invoked it repeatedly. It was a lie that could easily be exposed by anyone who took the trouble, as I have done here, to compare what Trotsky claimed was in the articles in *Humanité* and Soviet newspapers with what Trotsky claimed was in them. Therefore Trotsky took a significant risk in telling this "amalgam." Moreover, he told it repeatedly. It follows that this "amalgam" had to be very important to him for some reason.

The only explanation I can find that would account for his repeating this lie over and over again is Trotsky's stated tactic to "expose the scheme in advance." Trotsky must have raised this issue as a pre-emptive strike to ward off the charge that he believed would come sooner or later by making it appear "predictable" and therefore "obviously" false At length, Trotsky was indeed charged with it by Radek, Piatakov, and Sokol'nikov, and these men linked Trotsky's advocacy of "restoring capitalism" to his view that the opposition would have to make serious concessions to aggressive capitalist states in order to be able to take and hold power.

Trotsky vehemently denied having been in touch with Radek, Piatakov, and Sokol'nikov. But we know that here too Trotsky was lying – he had indeed been in contact with them. We know that Radek was telling the precise truth when he described receiving a letter from Trotsky at the end of February or beginning of March, 1932.[31] There is no reason to think that Radek did not tell the truth in the rest of his testimony as well.

Radek, Piatakov and Sokol'nikov linked Trotsky's alleged statements that they would have to "restore capitalism" to the need to collaborate with Germany and Japan. And it stands to reason that no plans to replace the Stalin leadership would make any sense without making some kind of advance agreement with Germany and Japan. These were the policies that were described in the January 1937 Trial as constituting a "restoration of capitalism."

We have a good deal of other evidence that Trotsky conspired with Germany and Japan.[32] I will identify and discuss yet more of this evidence in future books on Trotsky during the 1930s. Trotsky's "'restoration of capitalism' amalgam" is consistent with such a conspiracy. I conclude that this "amalgam" of Trotsky's *corroborates* the other evidence I have that Trotsky conspired with the Germans and Japanese.

---

[31] See Furr, Trotsky's Amalgams, Chapter 4; Furr, Moscow Trials, Chapter 4.
[32] See Furr, *Leon Trotsky's Collaboration with Germany and Japan.*

Conclusion

In raising time after time the false claim that Zinoviev and Kamenev had been accused of, confessed to, and been convicted of "plotting the restoration of capitalism," Trotsky was doing his best to defuse, through anticipation, the accusation he knew would sooner or later be leveled at himself. He knew this would be alleged against him because he himself had been advocating exactly the "restoration of capitalism" to the leadership of his Soviet-based followers for some time – at least since 1935, according to Radek, perhaps as early as 1933, according to Piatakov and Krestinsky. This hypothesis is consistent with a great deal of other evidence we now possess.

We have no reason to doubt the Soviet and non-Soviet evidence that Trotsky collaborated with Germany and Japan. Trotsky's denials cannot be taken seriously. Thanks to the research of Broué, Getty, and Holmström, we now know that Trotsky routinely lied whenever he thought it advantageous to do so. Trotsky's lies went far beyond denying the involvement in his conspiracy of individuals. He also lied about important issues of principle such as his willingness to enter a bloc with other oppositionists and his willingness to employ "individual terror," or assassination against Stalin and others.

Any demand that "conclusive evidence," a "smoking gun," be produced is simply a form of denial. In the case of a deeply conspiratorial organization as the opposition underground in the USSR necessarily had to be, one whose goal was to leave *no* evidence behind, we are forced to be content with composing a mosaic of *circumstantial* evidence. We possess even this circumstantial evidence only because (a) the Soviet Union came to an end and some documents from Soviet archives have become public, and (b) the "purging" of incriminating documents from the Harvard Trotsky archive was done imperfectly.

Absent these archival materials, Trotsky would still have formed a bloc with the Zinovievists and other opposition groups, would still have written Radek, Sokol'nikov, and others, and – I argue – would still have conspired with Germany and Japan. The defendants in the Moscow Trials would still have been telling the truth, and Trotsky would still have been lying, in those cases we can now verify. But we would not have had the evidence that this was so. We would have only the testimony from the Moscow Trials.

This is yet more evidence that the Moscow Trial testimony should be taken far more seriously when we *cannot* corroborate it, considering that it turns out to be truthful in those few examples where, by accident of history, we *can* check it. It also means that nothing Trotsky wrote during the 1930s about his own activities or the USSR should be accepted as true unless it can be independently verified. The standard of evidence should be uniformly applied, not adjusted in accordance with what supports dominant anticommunist narratives.

Chapter 5. Trotsky in *Biulleten' Oppozitsii*

Trotsky dated issue #42 of the *Biulleten' Oppozitsii* February 1935, only one month after the Kirov assassination issue #41 of January 1935. After the first few years of publication, it had become unusual for Trotsky to publish back-to-back issues of the B.O. For example, there had been only two issues during the whole of 1934. So why did Trotsky do so this time?

Three articles, comprising about two-thirds of this issue, were devoted to the Kirov murder and related matters, especially the January 1935 indictment and trial of Zinoviev, Kamenev, Safarov, and the rest of the men whose arrests Trotsky had mentioned in the previous issue. These three articles have been published in English translation in the volume *Writings of Leon Trotsky [1934-1935]*. I will analyze them here. They are:

* "Some Results of the Stalin Amalgam." (January 12, 1935)[1]

* "The Case of Zinoviev, Kamenev and Others." (January 16 – 18, 1935)

* "Everything Gradually Falls Into Place." (January 26, 1935)

Like the whole of the Kirov murder issue #41, these articles set forth Trotsky's "amalgam," what he claimed was his theory about what was really going on. In reality, they represent Trotsky's cover-up, his "smokescreen." At the very least, Trotsky and his Soviet-based supporters were in alliance with the Zinovievists who murdered Kirov.

In fact, we now have evidence that they were much more deeply involved in the murder than that, and Trotsky knew almost every-

---

[1] This article is also online at
https://www.marxists.org/archive/trotsky/1935/01/amalgam.htm where it is titled "A Trial Balance of the Stalin Amalgam."

thing about the Kirov murder. I will explore this question further in the third volume of my work on Trotsky in the 1930s.

Trotsky had decided not to reveal his ties to the Zinovievists, and through them to the Leningrad-based Zinovievist group that had murdered Kirov or to the bloc of Rights and Trotskyists, and Zinovievists. So he had to invent a fictitious version of events. While claiming that he was trying to deduce the truth of what was happening inside the USSR around the Kirov murder, in reality Trotsky was creating a false story that might accomplish several aims.

First, it would stand as his claim that he and his Soviet-based followers were innocent of Kirov's murder and of any thought of resorting to "terror." Second, it would demonize Stalin and his colleagues as bloodthirsty thugs who not only were using Kirov's murder to suppress anyone they considered a threat to their power but also may even have killed Kirov themselves.

Trotsky's alternative narrative would also serve to misdirect readers, get them to begin asking not, "Why is the Opposition using 'terror'?" but "Why is *Stalin* using 'terror'?" Therefore, it would serve as Trotsky's "cover" for the real conspiratorial activities of his Soviet-based followers.

It is worth noting that Trotsky never refers to anything his Soviet-based adherents really were doing. After all, if the "Left Opposition," the "Bolshevik-Leninists" (as Trotsky referred to his followers) were viewed by Stalin as such a threat, then they must have been doing something! But Trotsky never mentions any activity at all by Soviet-based Trotskyists. A discerning reader at the time would have wondered whether Trotsky's silence about his followers' activities might suggest that those activities – obviously clandestine ones -- were indeed what the Soviet prosecution alleged.

Ironically, therefore, it was not Stalin and the NKVD but Trotsky himself who had to fabricate what Trotsky liked to call "amalgams." Trotsky's "amalgams" are structured in a number of ways:

* He severely distorted what he has found in the Soviet or other communist press accounts.

* Some of his falsehoods serve as "straw men" – statements he falsely attributes to Soviet sources and which he can easily claim to "refute."

* Sometimes these falsehoods serve as "red herrings," permitting Trotsky to deflect his readers' attention from the real developments in the USSR and to fabricate imaginary "amalgams," fictions in which Stalin and his men are the villains while the Opposition are innocent of any unprincipled acts and are in fact doing nothing at all.

* Sometimes Trotsky simply lied outright about what these accounts say.

Trotsky also lied about his own activities and principles:

* He claimed that he always broke completely with "capitulators." We know today, from materials Getty discovered in the Harvard Trotsky Archive, that this was a lie: he did not break off with them. (Getty, TIE)

* He pretended to attack these same "capitulators" in print in what we now know was an attempt at a "cover" to disguise continued secret collaboration with them.

* He suppressed the truth about his real ties to the Zinovievists who were the subjects of the arrests and trials.

* He salted his presentation with anti-Stalin rumors and lies which he reported as fact.

"Some Results of the Stalin Amalgam" (January 12, 1935)

It is in this issue that Trotsky begins to set forth an "amalgam" that was destined to become for many years the "mainstream," or standard, version of the Kirov assassination: that it was Stalin who had had Kirov killed.

> 1. Таинственный консул оказался латышским консулом: наше предположение, что для амальгамы выбран маленький консул маленькой страны подтвердилось полностью. Но необходимость назвать консула – очевидно, под дипломатическим давлением – грозила опрокинуть амальгаму: кто же поверит, что консул Латвии **организует мировую интервенцию против СССР**?

Translated:

> 1. The mysterious consul has now turned out to be a Latvian consul; our supposition that a petty consul of a tiny nation would be chosen for the amalgam has been fully confirmed. However, it became necessary to name the consul – obviously because of diplomatic pressure – and this necessity threatened to blast the amalgam, for who would believe that a consul of Latvia is **the organizer of world intervention against the USSR**? (208)

In an essay titled "The Indictment" («Обвинительный акт») in B.O. #41 Trotsky had indeed said:

> ... консул представлял, надо думать, какое-нибудь совсем маленькое и захолустное государство: это безопаснее).

Translated:

> ... the consul represented, I suppose, some very small and provincial state: that would be safer).

The fact that even before the Latvian consult had been publicly identified Trotsky had "predicted" the consul would be from a very small country suggests that Trotsky knew this in advance. Trotsky's words "that would be safer" do not explain his remark. After all, the consul could easily have been Polish or German. We know today that Nikolaev, Kirov's assassin, had the address and phone number of the German consulate in his notebook. (Lenoe 258) Aside from the Baltics, there were simply no other "very small and provincial states" anywhere near the USSR. Indeed, the Latvian consul may have already initiated contact with Trotsky, as he told Leonid Nikolaev, Kirov's assassin, that he would.

Then comes a "straw man," designed to confuse and distract the reader. The *Humanité* text of the indictment mentions the word "consul" nine times, but never accuses him of being "the organizer of world intervention against the USSR." It is easy for Trotsky to ridicule this allegation as though the Soviet indictment had stupidly made it – unless some reader bothered to check the text of the indictment.

But any reader who did so would immediately see that Trotsky was lying. And that implies that Trotsky believed he had something important enough to hide to be worth the risk of exposure.

> 2. Группа Зиновьева была арестована по делу об убийстве Кирова. Обвинительный акт не заикается, между тем, ни об одном из арестованных в Москве зиновьевцев. Почему же все-таки они были арестованы?

Translated:

> 2. The Zinoviev group was arrested in connection with the Kirov assassination. Yet the indictment does not so much as let out a peep concerning a single one of the Zinovievists arrested in Moscow. But why then are they arrested? (208-209)

This too is a straw man, a distractor. The indictment Trotsky mentions is that of the *Leningrad* group of Zinovievists who were tried for murdering Kirov. The *Moscow* Zinovievist group, Zinoviev, Kamenev, and others, had been arrested because the Leningrad group of Zinovievist that had planned and carried out Kirov's murder was in touch with them. The Moscow-based Zinovievists were not indicted for the murder because the NKVD had found no evidence they were aware of it. (Such evidence was eventually found, but not until much later.)

3. В чем можно обвинить Зиновьева, Каменева и их друзей политически? В том, что они капитулировали.

Translated:

3. What charge, politically, may be brought against Zinoviev, Kamenev, and their friends? Their capitulation.

This too is a distractor – in this case, a "red herring." Trotsky is discussing the indictment of the Leningrad Zinovievist group for the Kirov murder. Then he asks this rhetorical question about the Moscow-based Zinovievist group who were not indicted and so, logically, were not mentioned in the indictment.

Trotsky, of course, knew that Zinoviev, Kamenev, Safarov, and other leading members of the bloc that he himself, Trotsky, had approved in 1932, had "capitulated" dishonestly. Their "capitulations" – renunciation of oppositional views and oaths to follow the Party line – were false. In the language of the Soviet investigators, they were guilty of "two-facedness" or "double-dealing" (*dvulichie, dvurushnichestvo*). Pierre Broué firmly stated that this was a common practice and that "everybody had known" that Smirnov and his group had been lying in their "capitulation" and that Safarov had been the first one to suggest this as a necessary tactic. (Broué POS 104) Naturally, Trotsky hid this fact from his readers.

Попытка связать большевиков-ленинцев с идеей интервенции имеет очень определенный исторический запах.

Translated:

There is a specific historical stench to this attempt at connecting the Left Opposition with the idea of intervention.[2]

Trotsky's accusation is a "straw man." The Leningrad Zinovievist group was indeed accused in the Soviet press (but not by the Prosecution) of trying to provoke foreign intervention:

> Cependant, ne comptant pas sur la réalisation de telles actions à « l'intérieur du pays », le groupe TABLAIT DIRECTEMENT SUR L'AIDE « DU DEHORS ," SUR L'INTERVENTION ARMEE ET L'AIDE DE CERTAINS ETATS ETRANGERS.[3]

Translated:

> However, not counting on the realization of such actions "inside the country" the group WAS COUNTING DIRECTLY ON AID "FROM OUTSIDE," ON ARMED INTERVENTION AND THE HELP OF CERTAIN FOREIGN STATES.

But Trotsky cannot point to any claims in the Soviet press linking the Left Opposition – Trotsky and his followers – to "intervention." In a previous chapter, I examined in more detail Trotsky's "amalgam" or false allegation that the Soviet investigators and prosecution – "Stalin" – were trying to connect him, Trotsky, with "foreign intervention."

The events of 1926 and 1917 consume all of points 4 and 5 of this article while saying nothing about the matter at hand. Perhaps Trotsky preferred to turn his readers' attention to these years, when he himself played an important role.

---

[2] At this point two paragraphs concerning the 1926 Opposition platform have been inserted into the English version. They are absent from the Russian original in B.O. #42.

[3] *Humanité*, December 28, 1934, p. 3 col. 3,, subhead ""Aidés par l'étranger!"

Все 14 обвиняемых по делу об убийстве Кирова оказались расстреляны. Все ли они участвовали в террористическом акте? Обвинительный акт отвечает на этот вопрос утвердительно, но не приводит и тени доказательства.

Translated:

The fourteen who were accused in connection with the Kirov assassination were all shot. Did they all participate in the terrorist act? The indictment answers this question in the affirmative, but it does not adduce even the semblance of proof.

This is a lie. Both the original indictment in the Kirov murder case, which had been published in *Pravda* on December 27, 1934, and even the abbreviated version in *Humanité* of December 28 which Trotsky explicitly cited, summarized a lot of evidence, as anyone who read them would know. This evidence is the confessions of several of the defendants, partial confessions of others, and mutual accusations by some defendants of others. I have put both the Russian text of the Indictment and the abbreviated French text from *Humanité* online. Matthew Lenoe has translated most of it into English, and I have published a criticism of Lenoe's omissions.[4]

As in the previous issue of B.O., Trotsky is taking a risk – namely, that his readers will not think to compare what he is writing with the text of the indictment.

Мы видели, с какой наглой и вместе трусливой тенденциозностью он впутывает в свой текст имя Троцкого, сознательно умалчивая о том, какие последствия имела провокация консула насчет "письма."

---

[4] Russian text of the Indictment: https://msuweb.montclair.edu/~furrg/research/obvin_zak_dec34.html ; Lenoe's partial text of the Indictment, in English translation, is in Lenoe, *The Kirov Murder and Soviet History*. New Haven: Yale University Press, 2010, 345-352. My critique of Lenoe's omissions is in Furr Kirov 210-217. For a hyperlink to the French text see note 6, below.

Translated:

> We have seen with what brazen and cowardly tenden-
> tiousness it has injected the name of Trotsky into its text
> and how deliberately it passes over in silence what hap-
> pened to the consul's provocation regarding the "letter."
> (210)

There are two falsehoods in this sentence:

* As in the previous issue of B.O., Trotsky says nothing about the "Trotskyite-Zinovievite bloc," although it is mentioned three times in the abbreviated indictment. This is a transparent, even an in-criminating omission. Anyone who read both texts would notice it and might wonder what the reason for this omission could be. Trotsky must have felt that remaining silent about the bloc was worth this risk. So the claim that "the name of Trotsky" was men-tioned "with brazen and cowardly tendentiousness" is designed only to confuse the reader.

* The Indictment does not "deliberately pass over in silence" the issue of the consul and letter to Trotsky at all. On the contrary, they are mentioned prominently:

> «Il dit qu'il pouvait établir **la liaison** avec Trotsky si je
> lui remettais une lettre du groupe à Trotsky.»

Translated:

> He said that he could establish **the contact** with Trotsky
> if I gave him a letter from the group to Trotsky.[5]

The French text clearly implies that the consul was not the first one to mention contact with Trotsky. The consul does not say "liai-son" (contact) but "**la** liaison" – "**the** contact," a contact previously

---

[5] "La Révolution Se Défend. L'acte d'accusation contre Nikolaiev..." *Humanité* December 28, 1934, p. 3 col. 2.

mentioned. The original Russian text of the indictment contains the same implication:

> При этом сказал, что установить связь с Троцким он может, если я вручу какое-либо письмо от группы к Троцкому.

Translated:

> He [the consul] also said that, as for establishing contact with Trotsky, he could do so if I should give him some kind of letter from the group to Trotsky.

The indictment never states that Nikolaev actually gave the consul such a letter. If the investigators had known that he did, the indictment would certainly have mentioned it. And the investigators could not interrogate or search the consul of a foreign country, as Trotsky knew. Here, as elsewhere, Trotsky was hoping that no one would bother to check what he wrote against the text of the indictment available in *Humanité*.

> Дело идет не о борьбе советской бюрократии против Троцкого и "троцкистов." Дело идет о моральной атмосфере мирового рабочего движения. Гнусная амальгама вокруг "консула," служившего, видимо, одновременно трем правительствам, принадлежит ныне к числу обычных, нормальных приемов сталинской бюрократии в борьбе за ее кастовые позиции.

Translated:

> What is here involved is not so much the struggle of the Soviet bureaucracy against Trotsky and the "Trotskyists" but the question of the moral atmosphere of the world working class movement. The vile amalgam constructed around the "consul," who apparently was in the simultaneous employ of three governments, stands today as one of a number of ordinary and normal measures utilized by the Stalinist bureaucracy in the struggle for its caste positions.

Understandably, Trotsky wanted to direct his readers' attention away from discussion of his and his followers' involvements with the Leningrad Zinovievist terrorists. This is the most likely explanation for his silence about the "Trotskyite-Zinovievite bloc." Clearly, it was not in Trotsky's interest to focus the readers' attention on the bloc.

The sentence about the consul is another "straw man." Trotsky later claimed that the Latvian consul had "given 5000 rubles for the organization of Kirov's murder." (227) This is a lie. What the indictment really stated was something quite different: that *it was Nikolaev who asked the consul for money* for the Leningrad Zinovievist group:

> «J'ai ensuite demandé au consul de nous prêter une aide matérielle, lui disant que nous lui rendrions l'argent prêté aussitôt que notre situation financière changerait.
>
> «A l'entrevue suivante, la troisième ou la quatrième au consulat, le consul m'informa qu'il était prêt à satisfaire à ma demande et me remit 5.000 roubles.

Translated:

> I then asked the consul to lend us material help and told him that we would return the money loaned to us as soon as our financial situation changed.
>
> At the next interview, the third or fourth at the consulate, the consul told me that he was ready to satisfy my request and handed me 5,000 rubles.

Nor does the indictment say anything at all about the consul being aware of an attempt to kill Kirov.

The "three governments" alleged by Trotsky would have been, besides Latvia, Hitler's Germany and the USSR, since Trotsky proposed that Kirov's murder was organization by the NKVD:

> Понадобилась новая версия: консул Латвии являлся на самом деле агентом Гитлера.

- "Некоторые итоги сталинской амальгамы,"

Translated:

> A new version was necessary: the consul of Latvia was at
> the same time an agent of Hitler.
>
> - "Some Results of the Stalin Amalgam," B.O. #42

Anyone who read the Indictment or the abbreviated French version in *Humanité* would know that neither the Soviet press nor the
Indictment against the Kirov defendants accused the Latvian consul of working with or for Germany.

Meanwhile, the notion that Stalin was involved in Kirov's murder
was another "red herring." Blaming Stalin for killing Kirov was yet
another example of "exposing the scheme in advance," of "getting
out in front" of the accusation that Trotsky could be reasonably
certain would be aimed before long at himself.

Trotsky includes his "peppery dishes" tale here:

> В 1921 г., предупреждая ближайших товарищей против
> избрания Сталина генеральным секретарем, Ленин
> говорил: "этот повар будет готовить только острые
> блюда."

Translated:

> In 1921, warning his most intimate comrades against
> electing Stalin as general secretary, Lenin said, "This
> cook will prepare only peppery dishes."

As I showed in Chapter One, this story too is a lie.

"The Case of Zinoviev, Kamenev and Others." (January 16 – 18, 1935)

Trotsky continues constructing his own "amalgam," or deliberately
false account, of the events in the USSR:

Их арестовали для амальгамы, т.-е. для установления связи между террористическим убийством и оппозицией, всякой вообще оппозицией, всякой вообще критикой, прошлой, настоящей и будущей. Их решились арестовать, потому что все казалось заранее рассчитано.

Translated:

> They [Zinoviev, Kamenev and 14 of their associates] were arrested with a view to an amalgam, that is to say, in order to establish a connection between the terrorist assassination and the Opposition, all opposition, all criticism in general, past, present or future. It was decided to arrest them when everything seemed to have been already settled. (213)

Trotsky knew from reading the abbreviated indictment as published in *Humanité* that the Kirov murder defendants had revealed the existence of the Trotskyist-Zinovievist bloc.[6] Therefore the connection between the terrorist murder and both the Zinovievist and the Trotskyist oppositions had already been established. But although he had personally approved its formation, Trotsky had decided to deny that the bloc existed. Consequently, we are dealing with Trotsky's own "amalgam," or false story, here.

Trotsky continues by elaborating his own "amalgam" of Stalin's involvement, via the GPU (NKVD), with Kirov's murder:

ГПУ было в курсе подготовлений террористического акта в Ленинграде. "Консул" выполнял данное ему поручение: он представлял соединительное звено амальгамы. Но действительный террорист, Николаев, в последний момент -- по соображениям конспирации -- оторвался, видимо, от своей собственной группы, в том числе и от входивших в нее агентов ГПУ. Раздался роковой выстрел. Он не входил в программу Сталина. Но это был риск

---

[6] I have put the text of the abbreviated Kirov indictment, from *Humanité*, December 28, 1934, p.3, online here: http://msuweb.montclair.edu/~furrg/research/kirov_indict_humanite1228.pdf

пре1дприятия. Киров пал жертвой. Агенты ГПУ
пострадали: старших сместили, младших расстреляли
вместе с террористами.

Translated:

> The NKVD was conversant with the preparations for the
> Leningrad terrorist act. The "consul" had carried out the
> task assigned to him; he was the link in the amalgam.
> The real terrorist, Nikolaev, however, it appears, at the
> last moment for conspiratorial reasons — detached him-
> self from his own group, including the agents of the
> NKVD who were playing a part in it The fatal shot rang
> out. It wasn't in Stalin's program. But that was the risk in
> the enterprise. Kirov fell victim. The NKVD agents paid
> for it: the higher officials were dismissed, the lower ones
> were shot together with the terrorists. ("The Case of Zi-
> noviev, Kamenev and Others," WLT 1934-35, 213)

This is all invention, more "smokescreen" and "red herrings." No
lower-ranking NKVD workers were shot together with Nikolayev's
group ("the terrorists"). There was never any evidence of contact
between the NKVD and the Latvian consul. There was never any
evidence of Stalin's involvement in Kirov's murder. Trotsky, of
course, knew that it was not Stalin but the bloc that had been
planning the assassinations of Kirov, Stalin, and others.

It is tempting to hypothesize that Trotsky may have known about
Iagoda's indirect involvement with the Kirov murder, of which we
know from Iagoda's pretrial confessions of 1937 as well as from
his testimony at the March 1938 Moscow Trial.[7] Iagoda discussed
with Radek his attempts to stop or at least minimize the repres-
sion of the underground Trotskyists in the aftermath of the Kirov

---

[7] Iagoda's important pretrial and trial confessions are fully discussed in Furr,
Kirov, Chapters 14 and 15.

murder. It is possible that Radek conveyed to Trotsky whatever he knew himself.

Trotsky repeats a falsehood from his article in B.O. #41:

> Пришлось Зиновьева-Каменева и их друзей выделить из процесса. Обвинительный акт по делу Николаева не упоминал о них ни словом;...

Translated:

> It was necessary to leave out from the trial the case of Zinoviev, Kamenev, and their friends. The indictment in the Nikolaev case said not one word about them... (214)

This is a lie. The Kirov indictment, including the abbreviated version in *Humanité,* did indeed mention Zinoviev, Kamenev, and the "groupe antisoviétique Zinoviev" numerous times. I have studied this lie of Trotsky's in a previous chapter.

Under the heading "17 January" Trotsky asserts that Bakaev, one of the defendants, "must have" testified under threat of being tried as one of Kirov's assassins. (217) This is an interesting statement by Trotsky.

Bakaev was indeed involved in Kirov's murder, as were Zinoviev and Kamenev. But Trotsky does not claim that Zinoviev and Kamenev had testified out of a threat of being tried as among Kirov's killers. Bakaev was in Moscow, as were Zinoviev and Kamenev. Along with Zinoviev, Kamenev, and others Bakaev was to be a defendant in the First Moscow Trial of August 1936. There Bakaev, like Zinoviev and Kamenev, admitted to involvement in the plan to kill Kirov. All three had been named by so many of their accomplices that further denial was pointless.

In the present study I demonstrate that Trotsky, whose strategy was to deny all accusations, sometimes made a statement that did not fit his fictive narration. A statement of this sort is a "tell," something that revealed more than he intended. In the light of what we know now about Trotsky's strategy of falsification, we can see that this remark of Trotsky's about Bakaev is such a "tell."

Under "18 January," Trotsky discusses the abbreviated text of the indictment against Zinoviev, Kamenev, Safarov et al. published the previous day, January 17, in *Humanité*.[8] Safarov began to testify, albeit in a veiled manner, about the formation of the Trotskyist-Zinovievist bloc in 1932, while not calling it a bloc. This was a threat to Trotsky, and he describes Safarov's quoted testimony as follows:

> Главный свидетель обвинения, Сафаров, почему то выделенный из процесса (роль этого субъекта в деле представляется крайне загадочной) показывает, что "контр-революционная" деятельность Зиновьева-Каменева и других была особенно активной в 1932 году! Но ведь за эту именно деятельность они и были исключены в 1932 году из партии и сосланы.

Translated:

> The chief witness for the prosecution, Safarov, whose case – we don't know why – was examined separately (the role of this individual in the affair appears most enigmatic), shows that the "counterrevolutionary" activity of Zinoviev, Kamenev, and the others was particularly intense in 1932! Yet it was precisely for this activity that in 1932 they were expelled from the party and deported. (218)

Trotsky's "deductions" here are pure misdirection. The fact that Safarov named the year 1932 must have been especially alarming to Trotsky. Sedov's 1932 letter to Trotsky explicitly identifies Safarov as someone who has not yet joined the bloc as it was being

---

[8] I have put the text of this abbreviated indictment, from *Humanité* January 17, 1935, p. 3 online at http://msuweb.montclair.edu/~furrg/research/zin-kam_indict_humanite011735.pdf

formed in 1932 but whose joining is expected shortly. But Safarov was not a Trotskyist. Perhaps Trotsky thought that Safarov might be more likely to identify Trotsky, Zinoviev, and others in order to save himself.

> Обвинительный акт ни словом не упоминает о связи этих обвиняемых с Николаевым.

Translated:

> The indictment does not mention by a single word the connection of the accused with Nikolaev. (220)

Another false statement. The abbreviated indictment in *Humanité* cites the contact between the Moscow group of Zinovievists and the Leningrad group that killed Kirov and of which Nikolaev was a part, as illustrated by this passage:

> L'instruction préliminaire établit que Zinoviev, Evdoki-mov, Guertik, Bakaev, Koukline, Kamenev, Charaov, Fe-dorov et Garchenine adhéraient au «Centre de Moscou», réunissant autour d'eux nombre des members les plus actifs de l'ancien groupement antisoviétique Zinoviev et **entretenant des rapports réguliers avec les members du groupe de Leningrad**, condamnés par le Collège militaire du Tribunal supreme de l'U.R.S.S. (affaire de l'assassinat de Kirov).
>
> Le « Centre de Moscou » ne se bornait pas seulement à l'entretien de rapports avec le groupe illégal de Lenin-grad et de certains de ses partisans dans 'd'autres villes, mais jouait un role de *centre politique dirigeant systématiquement,* au course d'un certain nombre d'années, l'activité contre-révolutionnaire secrète, **tant du groupe de Moscou que de celui de Leningrad.**

Translated:

> The preliminary instruction has established that Zino-viev and Gorshenin belonged to the "Moscow Center"

and brought together under them a number of the most active members of the old Zinoviev anti-Soviet grouping and **maintained regular contact with the members of the Leningrad group** condemned by the Military Collegium of the Supreme Court of the USSR (the Kirov assassination case).

The "Moscow Center" did not limit itself only to the maintenance of contact with the illegal Leningrad group and with certain of its members in other towns, but played the role of the *political center that systematically directed*, for a number of years, the secret counterrevolutionary activity of **both the Moscow group and of that of Leningrad**.

Once again, it appears that Trotsky was so intent upon constructing an "amalgam" that would direct attention away from the accusations of the Soviet court that he did not worry about the reactions of any reader who might compare what he wrote with the texts themselves.

Trotsky mentioned that the Kirov murder indictment cited the "platform" of 1926:

> Обвинительный акт по делу Николаева пытался, как мы помним, связать террористов с оппозиционной "платформой" 1926 года.

Translated:

> The indictment in the Nikolaev case tried, as we recall, to connect the terrorists with the "platform" of the 1926 Opposition. (150)

So it did – but, as I have shown in an earlier chapter, it also mentioned the "Trotskyite-Zinovievite bloc" four times (three in the French abbreviation). Trotsky remained silent about that.

Once again Trotsky falsely claimed that he has always broken with "capitulators":

> Пробовал ли Сталин при помощи военного суда дополнить работу консула и вырвать показания против Троцкого? Я не сомневаюсь в этом. Успеха он во всяком случае не имел. Принципом фракции большевиков-ленинцев всегда было рвать непримиримо с капитулянтами. Двойной бухгалтерии мы не допускаем.... Мы порвали в свое время с зиновьевцами так же решительно, как в прошлом году – с Раковским.

Translated:

> Did Stalin try to complete the consul's work by means of the military tribunal in order to extract declarations against Trotsky? I don't doubt it. In any case, he didn't succeed. The constant principle of the Bolshevik-Leninist faction is: break irreconcilably with capitulators. We do not allow double bookkeeping ... We broke in the past with the Zinovievists as resolutely as last year we broke with Rakovsky. (221)

Thanks to Broué's and Getty's discoveries in the Harvard Trotsky Archive, we know that this is a lie. Trotsky did not "break irreconcilably with capitulators." On the contrary: some, perhaps even all, such cases were a deception, designed to facilitate the continuation of clandestine opposition work inside the Party. Therefore, in his own words, Trotsky did indeed "allow double bookkeeping." His claim of principled oppositionism was a pose, undoubtedly essential for him to retain his non-Soviet followers and those Soviet followers who were not "in the know."

The following paragraph raises an interesting example: that of Khristian Rakovsky. At the March 1938 Moscow Trial, Rakovsky testified that he too had remained with Trotsky after making a false "capitulation":

> This took place in July or August 1932. One and a half years later, in February 1934, I sent a telegram to the Central

Committee of the C.P.S.U., saying that I had completely dis-
armed myself both ideologically and organizationally and
asked to be reinstated in the Party. This telegram was in-
sincere, I was lying. It was my deliberate intention to hide
from the Party and the government my association with
the Intelligence Service ever since 1924, and Trotsky's association with the Intelligence Service ever since 1926.
(1938 Trial 288-289)

Broué has admitted that "everybody" understood these "capitulations" to be a smokescreen. (POS 104) Trotsky's mentioning
Rakovsky in the same breath as Zinoviev and Kamenev strongly
suggests that Trotsky's supposed "break" with Rakovsky in 1934
was also a "cover" for the latter's continued secret Trotskyist
work. Trotsky confirms that his phony "break" with the false "capitulators" is his best defense:

Этот полный разрыв связей, политических и личных,
сделал невозможным – несмотря на помощь консула и
военного суда – успешное развитие амальгамы в сторону
большевиков-ленинцев.

Translated:

This complete rupture in personal and political relations
has made impossible – despite the help of a consul and a
military tribunal – future success in developing amalgams from the side of the Bolshevik-Leninists. (221)

This, of course, is another lie. Thanks to the research of Pierre
Broué and others, we know that there was no "break" with Zino-
viev, Kamenev, and the others in the bloc formed in 1932, or with
Radek and others to whom Trotsky wrote the same year.

This confirms Rakovsky's testimony that his "break" too was a
smokescreen. We now have much more primary source evidence
about Rakovsky's role in Trotsky's conspiracy, including about his
role as Trotsky's agent to the Japanese government. I discuss some
of it in Chapter 4 of *Leon Trotsky's Collaboration with Germany and*

Japan, and will include much more in a future book on Trotsky's conspiracies.

"Everything Gradually Falls Into Place." (January 28, 1935)

Here Trotsky continues the misdirection, or "amalgam," of his own. He writes:

> 30-го декабря 1934 года я высказывал твердую уверенность в том, что ГПУ было с самого начала в курсе подготовлявшегося террористического акта. Об этом неопровержимо свидетельствовало участие "консула," который мог быть только агентом ГПУ. Теперь мы имеем проверку. 23 января военный трибунал приговорил 12 ответственных ленинградских представителей ГПУ, во главе с их шефом Медведем к суровым карам: заключение от 2 до 10 лет! Приговор вменяет им в вину не более не менее, как тот факт, что "они были осведомлены о подготовлявшемся покушении на Кирова но обнаружилии преступную небрежность (!) и, не приняв необходимых мер охраны."

Translated:

> On December 30, 1934, I expressed the firm conviction that the GPU from the outset knew about the terrorist act that was being prepared. The participation of the "consul" who could only be an agent of the GPU, was the irrefutable evidence. Now we have the proof. On January 23, a military tribunal condemned twelve responsible representatives of the GPU in Leningrad, with, at their head, their chief, Medved, to hard labor: two to ten years' imprisonment! The sentence on them was for the charge that, no more, no less, "they were aware of the attempt being prepared against Kirov but showed criminal negligence (!) in not taking the necessary security measures." (223)

Trotsky's text is so close to the text in *Pravda* that Trotsky must
have had access to the Soviet paper. I have reproduced below the
words in *Pravda* of January 23, 1935, concerning the sentencing of
the NKVD men with Trotsky's words in his article dated January
26. Trotsky wrote:

> ...они были осведомлены о подготовлявшемся покушении
> на Кирова...

The text in *Pravda* of January 23, 1935 reads thus:

> ...располагая сведениями о готовящихся покушениях на
> тов. Сергея Мироновича Кирова...

Trotsky's language:

> ...но обнаружилии преступную небрежность...

The text in *Pravda:*

> ...проявили ... преступную халатность...

Trotsky's language:

> ...не приняв необходимых мер охраны.

The text in *Pravda:*

> ...не приняли необходимых мер охраны.

These passages prove that Trotsky had access to *Pravda* within a
day or two of its publication in the USSR. Trotsky's words either
echo those of the *Pravda* article precisely or are a very close para-
phrase. Trotsky must have read the *Pravda* article himself or had
someone read it to him while he made notes.

Here Trotsky was continuing his attempt to deflect attention away
from the involvement of the "Trotskyite-Zinovievite bloc" onto another – any other – target, by falsely asserting that NKVD men
were among the 14 executed for the Kirov murder; that the NKVD,
and by extension Stalin, were involved in the Kirov murder.

Trotsky concludes with phrases that are full of irony for us today:

> Революционный террор не нуждается в маскировке, ибо он находит непосредственное оправдание в сознании народных масс.

Translated:

> Revolutionary terrorism does not need a mask because it finds its immediate justification in the consciousness of the popular masses. (228)

We know from sources outside the USSR that Trotsky did indeed sanction the use of "terror," both from Sedov's words to Zborowski and from Trotsky's bloc with the Rights, who according to Jules Humbert-Droz were already planning Stalin's assassination in 1928. Like his declarations of permanent "break" with "capitulators" Trotsky's insistence in denouncing "terror" is more "cover" for his machinations.

Concerning Stalin's "amalgams" Trotsky wrote:

> Потребность в амальгамах возникает с того момента, когда бюрократия поднимается над революционным классом, как правящая каста, со своими особыми интересами, тайнами и махинациями.

Translated:

> The need for amalgams emerges when a bureaucracy rises above the revolutionary class as a privileged caste, with its special interests, secrets, and machinations. Fearing for its power and its privileges, the bureaucracy is compelled to deceive the people. (228)

What becomes of this analysis when we realize that it was not Stalin who was forging "amalgams" – false stories – but Trotsky himself? Moreover, on the evidence we now have, Stalin and the Soviet prosecutors had not fabricated anything. They were really trying to find out what was going on, trying to solve the crime.

Posing as a champion of the truth, Trotsky denounces Stalin's "amalgams," or deliberate falsifications. Meanwhile, it was *Trotsky* who was creating "amalgams" to disguise his real activities. Ironically, it was not Stalin but Trotsky himself who felt "compelled to deceive the people." Trotsky really held a mirror up to himself with that analysis.

On the evidence we have today, it is clear that the Stalin-era Soviet investigators did solve the Kirov murder.[9] Further investigation into the murder eventually led the NKVD to discover the bloc of Oppositionists – Zinovievists, Trotskyists, Rightists, and others – who were the defendants in all three of the public Moscow Trials of 1936, 1937, and 1938.

With the following words, Trotsky was also positioning himself to declare any future revelations by the NKVD and Soviet prosecutors as even larger fabrications:

> *Сталину необходимо прикрыть сорвавшиеся амальгамы новыми, более широкого масштаба и более успешными.* Нужно встретить их во всеоружии! Борьба против диких расправ над марксистской оппозицией в СССР неотделима от борьбы за освобождение мирового пролетарского авангарда от растлевающего влияния сталинских агентов и сталинских методов. Ни один честный пролетарский революционер не смеет молчать. Из всех политических фигур самой презренной является фигура Понтия Пилата.

Translated:

> *Stalin is forced to cover up the unsuccessful amalgams with new, broader and more successful ones.* We must meet them well armed. The struggle against the ferocious repressions against the Marxist opposition in the USSR is inseparable from the struggle for the liberation

---

[9] See Furr, Kirov. This is the inescapable conclusion from a careful study of all the evidence now available.

of the world proletarian vanguard from the influence of Stalinist agents and Stalinist methods. Not one honest revolutionary proletarian ought to be silent. Of all political figures, the most despicable is Pontius Pilate. (228; Emphasis in the original.)

At this point we should recall that Trotsky's principal tactic in covering up the bloc and his own activities was to "expose the scheme in advance." In his first article on the Kirov murder in B.O. #41 Trotsky had written:

> There is only one way to forestall en route the amalgams that are in preparation: *Expose the scheme in advance.* The Stalinists are trying to mold the public opinion of the world police towards expulsions, extraditions, arrests, and other more decisive measures. The Leninists must prepare the public opinion of the world proletariat for these possible events. In this case, as in others, it is necessary to speak out openly about what is; that is also the aim of the present article. ("The Stalinist Bureaucracy and the Assassination of Kirov")

Trotsky knew then – and we know now – that it was he himself, not the Soviet prosecution ("Stalin"), that was cooking up a false story or "amalgam" concerning Kirov's murder. Trotsky also suspected that the NKVD investigation would uncover more details of his own followers' activities, and therefore that more accusations against him would be forthcoming in the future.

Once he had begun to deny that the bloc with Zinoviev, Kamenev, and others existed, Trotsky had no choice but to compose a false account of the Kirov murder while pretending to be deducing what had really happened. The obvious tactic was to turn the tables and blame Stalin for Kirov's murder, and then blame Stalin again for trying to pin Kirov's murder on the real culprits, the bloc, including himself, Trotsky.

For the rest of his life, Trotsky continued to falsely claim that the Moscow Trials were a frame-up and that all the defendants including himself were its innocent victims. In a great historical irony, Trotsky's "amalgam" was to become the most influential account of Kirov's murder. Of course, Trotsky's followers accepted it. But the central event in its further development was Nikita Khrushchev's "Secret Speech" of February 25, 1956, when Khrushchev said:

> It must be asserted that to this day the circumstances surrounding Kirov's murder hide many things which are inexplicable and mysterious and demand a most careful examination.

In 1963 the Shvernik Commission appointed by Khrushchev to find evident for the "rehabilitations" of the Moscow Trials victims and many others, suggested that Stalin was behind Kirov's murder. In conformity with Khrushchev's goals, the Commission concluded:

> Никакого «Антисоветского право-троцкистского блока» в действительности не существовало ... (RKEB 2, 630)

Translated:

> No "Anti-Soviet Right-Trotskyist bloc" existed in reality...

This report was not published until 1994, after the end of the Soviet Union. But in the late 1980s it was studied and used by Gorbachev's men.

Aleksandr Iakovlev, a Politburo member and Gorbachev's chief for ideology, ordered an attempt to find evidence that Stalin was behind Kirov's murder. Iakovlev's high-level commission reluctantly concluded that there was no such evidence. So they settled for a compromise solution: they claimed that Nikolaev had been a "lone gunman," that there had never been a bloc, and that Stalin had used Nikolayev's crime to "frame" innocent people whom he thought were against him.

Thanks to the Harvard Trotsky Archive, we know today that the bloc did exist. The Shvernik Commission's, and Iakovlev's, reports are as phony, as deliberately dishonest, as the version by Trotsky on which, through Khrushchev, they were ultimately based. This story, which originated in Trotsky's need to deny and conceal his conspiracy, has become the canonical version of the Kirov murder.

Conclusion

Our research concerning Leon Trotsky has produced significant and complementary results:

* In *The Moscow Trials as Evidence* we determined that the defendants in the Moscow Trials were not innocent persons compelled to falsely testify by the investigation (NKVD) or prosecution. They said what they intended to say.

We determined this by verifying, with independent primary source evidence, a number of the statements made in testimony by Moscow Trials defendants. In the few cases where we can prove a defendant lied, he did so to further the conspiracy of which he was a part and/or in an attempt to protect himself, not to incriminate himself or to placate the prosecution.

* In the present book we have demonstrated that Leon Trotsky lied a great deal during the 1930s. It is fair – accurate -- to say that, concerning the Soviet Union and the Stalin leadership, Trotsky wrote little else except lies. Many of those lies are directly related to the accusations made against him by the defendants and the prosecution at the three Moscow Trials.

Other of Trotsky's lies concern the aftermath of the murder of Sergei Kirov in December 1934, an event that eventually led investigators to uncover the bloc of Trotskyists, Zinovievists, Rightists, and other Oppositionists, which Trotsky had approved and in which his secret Soviet-based supporters participated along with other oppositionists, including those who had killed Kirov.

We have determined that Trotsky lied so frequently and about so many things that *nothing* he wrote about the Soviet Union after the end of 1934 – the date of his first essays on the Kirov murder – represents what he himself really thought.

Trotsky lied in two basic ways. First, he denied any role in the conspiracies of which he was accused: with his own followers and other oppositionists within the Soviet Union; with foreign governments; with the German military; with the Red Army leaders. He denied the existence of the bloc of Trotskyists, Zinovievists, Rights, and other oppositionists. He denied having contact with a number of persons with whom we now know he did have contact.

Second, Trotsky chose the strategy of claiming that he would "expose the scheme in advance." It is asking too much of coincidence to think that Trotsky really did "predict" that the bloc members, including his own supporters and himself, would be accused of these things. The only explanation for these so-called predictions that is consistent with the evidence we now possess is that Trotsky knew that these accusations would eventually be forthcoming. Sooner or later, some of the bloc members would confess to them. So he anticipated them in order to make them seem so false they were "predictable."

Trotsky's declared strategy of "exposing the scheme in advance" is a "tell." His supposed "predictions" actually "telegraph" to us confirmation of some of the actions that Trotsky really had engaged in. Just as we know that the confessions of the Moscow Trials defendants are genuine, so we also know that Trotsky's denials are not reliable, because we can disprove many of his denials, and because Trotsky lied whenever he considered it expedient to do so.

During the investigation of the Kirov murder Trotsky claimed that he could "predict" that his name would be raised, when he knew that it would be because of his and his supporters' participation in the bloc with the Zinovievists.

Trotsky claimed that Zinoviev and Kamenev were charged with plotting "armed intervention" and the "restoration of capitalism." In reality, they were not charged with either. But Trotsky had advocated both. He could reasonably assume that he himself and his followers would be charged with these crimes sooner or later, as eventually happened.

In a conspiracy such as Trotsky's we can expect to find little or no *material* evidence. Conspirators do their best to leave no physical trace of their conspiracy. We have long had a great deal of *testimonial* evidence in the confessions of the Moscow Trials defendants. Having verified many details of the Moscow Trials confessions from independent sources, we can now accept the Moscow Trials testimony concerning Trotsky's conspiracies with a high degree of confidence. As additional confirmation we now have Trotsky's "predictions." They dovetail nicely with the later accusations against him.

It appears that in lying Trotsky acted from several motives:

* to cover up the activities of his followers in the Soviet Union;

* to preserve his image before his followers and on the world stage as a principled revolutionary and the true follower, by rights the heritor, of Lenin;

* to maintain a posture of non-involvement in politics, necessary to preserve his ability to find countries which would let him live there as an exile;

* above all, to maintain and continue his conspiracies against the Soviet leadership, in hopes of returning to power within the USSR.

The reality was very different from Trotsky's false accounts. His former followers testified at the Moscow Trials that Trotsky was

* advocating the murder of Stalin and other Soviet leaders;

* organizing the sabotage of Soviet industry and transportation;

* conspiring with Germany and Japan either to support a coup d'état against the Stalin regime or to stimulate mutiny within the Soviet military in support of German and Japanese attacks, thereby facilitating the overthrow of the Stalin regime and the assumption of power by the bloc and by Trotsky himself.

In the present volume we have cited good evidence of these activities by Trotsky, including evidence that corroborates the Moscow Trials testimony. We will examine yet more such evidence in a future study.

Denial

Soviet history is so politicized, and opinions about Soviet history so impassioned, that many readers will reject the results of this study not out of rational evaluation and criticism of the evidence, but out of simple denial thinly disguised by faulty reasoning.

For anticommunists and Trotskyists it is unthinkable that the Moscow Trials testimony should have turned out to be, on the whole, reliable. This fact invalidates what we have called the "anti-Stalin paradigm" of Soviet and world history. In the service of anticommunism, and of the cult around the figure of Trotsky, anticommunists and Trotskyists will continue to deny the truth as demonstrated by primary source evidence and sound analysis.

Nevertheless, we look forward to criticism from all quarters. Dishonest or incompetent criticism will expose the dishonesty and incompetence of those who employ it. Good, incisive, logical, and above all, *evidence-based* criticism will help to advance the cause of discovering the truth about Soviet history. Hopefully, such honest and competent criticism will also provide correctives that we can use to improve subsequent editions of this work.

In 2017 I published Volume Two of my Trotsky studies: *Leon Trotsky's Collaboration with Germany and Japan.* In that book I examine some of the large body of primary source evidence now available, mainly from formerly closed Soviet-era archives, that bear on Trotsky's conspiracies, including: important confirmation of Trotsky's conspiracies with Japan; further details of Trotsky's promotion of "terror" (assassination) and sabotage within the Soviet Union; details concerning; some details about Iurii Piatakov's secret flight to Norway in December, 1935, to consult with Trotsky; and much else.

My plan is to write more books in which I will analyze recently-released documents from the former Soviet archives that bear on Trotsky's conspiracies, including important confirmation of Trotsky's conspiracy with Japan; further details of Trotsky's promotion of "terror" and sabotage; more details concerning Piatakov's secret flight to Norway in December 1935; and much else. I will again draw upon primary documents, critically analyzed with appropriate scholarly skepticism, to further examine Trotsky's lies about his own activities and those of his adherents.

Recognition of the fact that Trotsky was indeed guilty of the serious charges made against him at the Moscow Trials necessitates a radical reinterpretation of the high politics in the Soviet Union during the 1930s. I have begun to re-examine this history in a number of recent books, including *Khrushchev Lied*, *The Murder of Sergei Kirov*, *Yezhov vs Stalin*, and *Stalin Waiting For ... The Truth*.

Appendix: Documents

(Note: I had originally intended to put many of the important archival documents cited in this book into this Appendix. But doing so would make this book, already longer than I had planned, much longer still.

I plan to include more documents in a following volume, to be published in late 2019 or early 2020.)

Document 1. Sedov to Trotsky 1932 Trotsky Arch. 4782

[Блок] организован. В него вошли <u>зиновьевцы,</u>
группа <u>Стэн-Ломинадзе</u> и <u>троцкисты</u>
(бывшие «_____». Группа Сафар.
Тархан. формально еще не вошла – они
стоят на слишком крайней позиции; войдут
в ближайшее время. – Заявление З. и К. об их
величайшей ошибке в 27 г. было сделано при
переговорах с нашими о блоке, непосредственно перед
высылкой З и К. –

Провал группы И.Н., Преобр. и Уф. (эти трое
входили в центр) был сделан каким то полу-
сумасшедшим, больным человеком. Его арестовали
случайно, -- он начал выдавать. Вряд ли у ИН и др.
нашли материалы («троцк. литература») за несколько
дней до ареста ИН говорил нашему информатору:
Х начал выдавать, я жду ареста со дня на день.
Он был подготовлен благодаря наличию <u>своего</u>
Морковкина, доставлявшего всю информац.
К сожалению его ИН. не успел передать. –

Информатор сообщает, что никаких провалов

едущих из-заграниц., вообще связанных с
заграницей <u>не</u> было.
Если есть очень важные вопросы – то
телеграфно до четверга (то же указания).

Провал «бывших» большой удар, но заводские
связи сохранялись.

Письмо № 2 получено по почте (хим).
2. Больш. информац. – лично. И та и друг.
от Веттера (помнишь). Молодец!

За последнее время в Р. уехало трое. Скоро жду
2^x. Пересланы «маленькие.» Организац. этих
поездок, их использован., передача и пр. требовало
в каждом случае многих часов обсуждения и работы,
иногда почта «ювелирной» (расскажу при случае).
Часто надо не только «инструктировать,» но и
прежде всего убедить. Никто (за 1 исклю-

———————

1 исключением) не шел сам, надо было найти при-
притянуть. Я имею сейчас постоян. «агента»
в Берлине, который иногда ездит. Отно-
шусь к нему с абсолют. доверием.

Из всех поездок туда ни одна не совершилась
«сама собою.» Я об этом всем пишу с
единственной целью уточнить вопрос
о моей судьбе под этим углом зрения.

Мой отъезд из Евр. будет фактически значать
ликвидац. связей; максимум, что можно
сохранить это часть односторонней пере-
писки от туда. Это же мнение моск.

друзей, находящихся в уныние « . Они
«считают», что мне необходимо оставаться в Е.

Создающееся положение ставит перед мною вопрос
не попытаться ли мне нелегально остаться
в Евр. (Brl или Париже наезшая в Brl), если не
дадут визы? Мнение. Паспорт у меня есть.

Во всяком случае отсутствие как бы то ни было
серезных связей во Фр. и Вене, видимо
поставит проблему так: Турц. или нелегальн.

Нелегальн. вопросы немецк. организации.   1) и важнейшее: создание
нелегальной типогр. в Берлине (в Лейнц. и Гамб. есть). купить
пока не трудно: 400-600 (maxim) марок, - но нет денег. Трудности
в установке, в помещании. Найти его наша главная забота. Пото[му]
нужны деньги. (также стоит вопрос с конфер. немецк. – по[ка]
нет денег; но Париж обещал). 2) Нелегальн. бюро (центр) [в]
Берлине удастся устроить хорошо. Мы имеем абсолютно
чистого т-ща Kaufmann'a из R., который откроет комерч.
бюро с представительством разных иностранн. фирм. Он собирает
сейчас эти представительства. Бюро, следов., не будет даже
фиктивным. Один из членов центра будет работать в бюро,
как служащ. Здесь будет явка, и пр. (для самого узко круга
разумеется)

3) В смысле заграничной базы мы ориентируемся на R
(Рейхенберг). 3 ½ - 4 часа езды от Brl, группа в 7-8
очень преданных людей, состоятельных. Легкая граница
(автомобили у сочувствующих). Там можно скрыться,
издавать газету для доставки в Герм. и пр.

Проявляйте химию утюгом – это скорее
Прошу подтвердить получение химии – письма.

English Translation:

[The bloc] has been organized. In it have entered the Zinovievists,
the Sten-Lominadze group and the Trotskyists
(former "capitulators"). The group of Safar.
Tarkhan. has not formally entered yet – they
stand on too extreme a position; they will enter
in a very short time. – The declaration of Z. and K. concerning their
enormous mistake in '27 was made during
negotiations with our people concerning the bloc, immediately before the exile of Z and K. –

The downfall of the group of I.N., Preobr. and Uf. (these three
were the center) was done by some half-
insane, sick person. They arrested him
by chance, – he began to name names. It is unlikely that they
found materials ("Trotsk. literature") on IN and others. Several
days before his arrest IN said to our informer:
X has begun to name names, I await arrest any day.
He was prepared thanks to the presence of <u>his</u>
Morkovkin, who brought all the informat.
Unforunately IN did not have time to transfer it. –

Informer says that <u>no</u> downfalls of those who are going abroad, of
those connected generally with abroad, have taken place.
If there are very important questions – then
by telegraph before Thursday (the same instructions).

The downfall of the "former" is a great blow, but factory
contacts are being preserved.

Letter No. 2 received by mail (chem).
2. Big informat. – personally. Both
from Vetter (remember). Great guy!

Recently three have departed for R. I await
2 soon. The "small ones" have been transferred. The organiz. of
these trips, their use, transfer etc. demanded
in each case many hours of discussion and work,
sometimes the post of "the jewelry" (I'll tell you when I have a
chance).
Often I had not only to "instruct," but also
above all to convince. No one (with one excep-)

––––––––––

1 exception) went alone, it was necessary to find and re-
recruit. I now have a permanent "agent"
in Berlin, who sometimes travels. I trust
him absolutely.

Of all the trips there not one was completed
"by itself." I write about all this for the
sole purpose of defining the question
of my own future from this point of view.

My departure from Eur. will in reality mean
the liquidation of my contacts; the maximum that could
be preserved is a part of the one-sided correspondence from there. That is the opinion of the Mosc.
friends who are dejected. They
"consider," that it is essential for me to stay in E.

The situation that is being created places before me the question
of whether I need to try to remain illegally in Eur. (Brl or Paris
with easy travel to Brl), if they
do not grant me visas. Opinion. I do have a passport.

In any case the absence of any kind of
serious connections in Fr. and Vienna, obviously
poses the problem thus: Turk. or illegal.

The illeg. questions of the Germ. Organization. 1) the most important: creation
of an illegal typogr. in Berlin (in Leipz. and Hamb. there <u>are</u>). To
buy one
is for the time being not hard: 400-600 (maxim) marks, – but
there's no money. Difficulties
in arrangement, in living quarters. To find it is our main concern.
Theref.
we need money. (same situation with question of Germ. Confer. –
for now
there's no money, but Paris has promised). 2) Illeg. buro (center)
[in]
Berlin has been successfully set up. We have an absolutely
pure c-rad Kaufmann from R., who will open a commerc.
buro with representation of various foreign firms. He is now preparing
these representations. The buro, consequen., will not even be a
fictional one. One of the members of the center will work in the
buro
as an employee. Here there'll be a hideout, etc. (for a very narrow
circle, of course)

3) In the sense of a base abroad we are focusing our attention on
R. (Reichenberg). 3 ½ -4 hours of travel from Brl, a group of 7-8
very devoted, well-off people. An easy border
(sympathizers have autos). There people can be concealed,
publish a newspaper for delivery to Germ. etc.

Bring out the chemical with an iron – it's faster
Please confirm receipt of the chemical – letter.

Document 2. Zborowski - Sedov on Killing Stalin, on Sedov's dissolution - Russian

Costello & Tsarev, *Deadly Illusions* p. 283 – Jan 22, 1937, & Feb 11, 1937, dispatches translated. Jan 23, 1937, remark translated in n. 44, p. 469.

Exactly the same texts, with Russian original, in Tsarev & Kostello, *Rokovye Illiuzii*, p. 169/322-3, and n. 44 p. 273/531

---

8 февраля 1937

22 января Л. Седов во время нашей беседы, у него на квартире, по вопросу о 2-м московском процессе и роли в нем отдельных подсудимых (Радека, Пятакова и др.) заявил: <u>Теперь колебаться нечего. Сталина нужно убить</u>"

Для меня это заявление было настолько неожиданным, что я не успел на него никак реагировать. Л. Седов тут же перевел разговор на другие вопросы.

23 января Л. Седов, в присутствии моем а также Л. Эстриной, бросил фразу такого же содержания как и 22-го. В ответ на это его заявление, Л. Эстрина сказала «Держи язык за зубами». Больше к этому вопросу не возвращались.

M Zborowski

С 1936 г. «сынок» не вел со мной разговоров о терроре. Лишь недели две-три тому назад, после собрания группы «сынок» снова заговорил на эту тему. В первый раз он только старался «теоретически» доказать, что терроризм не противоречит марксизму. «Марксизм - по словам сынка – отрицает терроризм постолько, посколько условия классовой борьбы не благоприпятствует терроризму, но бывают такие положения, в которых терроризм необходим." В следующий раз «сынок» заговорил о терроризме, когда я пришел к нему на квартиру работать. Во время читки газет «Сынок» сказал, что так как весь режим в СССР держится на Сталине, то достаточно убить Сталина, чтобы все развалилась. Эту мысль он высказывал и раньше, но до последнего раза он никогда ее так четко не формулировал. В этот последний раз он неоднократно возвращался к этому, и особенно тщательно подчеркивал необходимость убийства тов. Сталина.

В связи с этим разговором «сынок» спросил меня боюсь ли я смерти вообще и способен ли я был совершить террористичесий акт. На мой ответ что все это зависит от необходимости и целесообразности, сынок сказал, что я не совсем верно понимаю, что такое «настоящий» террорист и начал мне объяснять какими должны быть люди подходящие для исполнения терактов.

Переходя к тактике террора он остановился на кадрах, считая, что это основное. Террорист – по словам сынка – должен всегда быть готовым к смерти, смерть должна быть для террориста ежедневной реальностью, причем эту тезу он иллюстрировал примером психологии народовольцев. Причем при этом он бросил реплику, что я – по его мнению – человек слишком мягкий для такого рода дел.

Разговор на этим внезапно был прекращен появлением соседки, и после он не возобновился.

М Зборовский

11.II. 1938

_____

ВЫПИСКА ИЗ ПИСЬМА ГАММЫ

От 23-го июля 1937 года.

Мак и Сынок. По случаю рождения своего сына, Мак пригласил Сынка к себе на обед. Сынок просидел весь день за бутылкой у Мака, и крепко выпил. В этот вечер Соседка ждала Сынка для работы у него на дом. После Мака, с 6-ти и до 11 часов вечера, Сынок таскал Мака по разным кабакам Монпарнасса, и когда Мак с ним попрощался, Сынок вместо того, чтобы поехать домой, крепко выпивший пошел в публичный дом, прежде чем вернуться домой, где его ждала Соседка.

Сынок, выпив не терял сознания, но сильно расчувствовался. Он извинялся перед Маком и почти со слезами просил у него прощения за то, что в начале их знакомства он подозревал его в том, что он агент ГПУ. Эти свои подозрения он объяснял тем, что в прошлом, в свой берлинский период, к нему ГПУ неоднократно подсылало своих агентов и пр.

Под конец в процессе своих «откровений», Сынов говорил, что борьба оппозиции еще с самого начала в Союзе была безнадежна, и что в успех этой борьбы никто не верил. Что он еще в 1927 г. потерял всякую веру в революцию, и теперь он ни во что не верит вообще, что он вообще пессимист. Работа и борьба, которые ведутся теперь, являются простым механическим продолжением прошлого. В жизни для него основное – это женщины и вино. Он также любит игру на деньги.

Рассказывал, как находясь в Монтекарло Жанна не давала ему больше 50 франков в день, которые он сразу же проигрывал в рулетку. У него мечта поехать с деньгами в Монте-Карло

Накануне этого вечера Сынок жаловался Маку, что трудно с деньгами. Когда они пошли вечером в кабак, Сынок, уже сильно выпивший, расплачиваясь, вытащил бумажник, и Мак увидел, что в нем лежит солидная пачка тысячефранковых билетов – Сынок разменял тысячу франков, чтобы расплатиться.

После этого случая Сынок начал таскать почти ежедневно Мака выпивать. Каждый раз, как Мак встречался с Сынком, даже у него на дому, Сынок вытаскивал бутылку вина, не стесняясь; как это было раньше. Как видно он решил сделать Мака своим собутыльником. Мак ведет себя осторожно в время этих выпивок, он вообще крепок в этом отношении, и кроме того – выпивая сам рюмку, наливает Сынку три.

Верно: (Алексеев)

———————————

English Translation:

February 8, 1937

On January 22 L. Sedov, in our conversation at his apartment on the question of the Second Moscow Trial and the role in it of individual defendants (Radek, Piatakov, et al.) stated: "Now there is no reason to hesitate. Stalin must be killed."

For me this statement was so unexpected that I did not manage to react to it in any way. L. Sedov immediately turned the conversation on to other questions.

On January 23 L. Sedov, in my presence and also that of L. Estrina, said something of the same content as that of the 22nd. In answer to his statement L. Estrina said: "Keep your mouth shut." We did not return to this question any more.

———————————

Since 1936, "Sonny" has not talked with me about terror. Only two or three weeks ago, after a meeting of the group, "Sonny" began to speak again on this theme. The first time he tried only to "theoretically" prove that terrorism does not contradict Marxism. "Marxism" – in "Sonny's" words – rejects terrorism only insofar as the conditions of the class struggle are unfavorable for terrorism, but there exist conditions under which terrorism is essential." The next time "Sonny" began to talk about terrorism when I arrived at his apartment to work. While he was reading newspapers "Sonny" said that since the whole regime in the USSR is held up by Stalin, it would be enough to kill Stalin for it all to fall apart. He had expressed this idea earlier as well but until this last time he had never formulated it so clearly. This last time he returned repeatedly to this subject, and emphasized the necessary of the murder of com[rade] Stalin with especial care.

In connection with this conversation "Sonny" asked me whether I feared death in general and whether I would be able to carry out an act of terror. At my answer that this all depends on whether it is essential and expedient, Sonny said that I did not understand correctly what a "real" terrorist is and began to explain to me what kind of qualities people suitable for carrying out terrorist acts should be.

As far as the tactics of terror he stopped at the question of cadre. He considered that the fundamental thing. A terrorist, in Sonny's words, must always be prepared for death, death must be a daily reality for a terrorist, and he then illustrated this thesis by the example of the psychology of the Narodovoltsy. Thereupon he threw out the remark that I, in his opinion, am too soft a person for this kind of business.

The conversation on this subject was suddenly cut short by the appearance of Neighbor, and it did not start up again afterwards.

M. Zborowski

II.II. 1938

Excerpt from Letter of Gamma of July 23, 1937

Mak and Sonny [= Zborowski and Sedov]. On the occasion of the birth of his son Mak invited Sonny to his place for dinner. Sedov sat the whole day drinking at Mak's and got seriously drunk. That evening Neighbor [= Estrine] was expecting Sonny at his home to do work. After Mak, from 6 till 11 in the evening, Sonny dragged Mak around to various bars in Montparnasse, and when Mak said goodnight to him Sonny, instead of going home and seriously drunk, went into a brothel rather than return home where Neighbor was waiting for him.

Sonny drank heavily without losing consciousness, but became very sentimental. He apologized to Mak, and almost in tears asked for forgiveness for the fact that at the beginning of their acquaintance he suspected him of being an agent of the GPU. He explained his suspicions by the fact that in the past, in his Berlin period, the GPU had repeatedly tried to send its agents to him, etc.

Towards the end in the process of his "revelations" Sonny said that the struggle of the opposition had been hopeless from the very beginning, and that no one believed that this struggle would succeed. That he had lost all belief in the revolution already in 1927, and that now he did not believe in anything at all, that he was a pessimist about everything. The work and the struggle that was going on now were a simple mechanical continuation of the past. The main thing in life for him was women and wine. He also liked to gamble for money.

He told a story about how, when they were in Monte Carlo Jeanne [Sedov's wife] would not give him more than 50 francs a day, which he would always lose immediately playing roulette. He dreamed of going to Monte Carlo with money.

The day before this particular evening Sonny complained to Mak that he was hard up for money. When they went in the evening to a bar Sonny, already seriously drunk, pay the tab and took out a wallet, and Mak saw in it a solid packet of thousand-frank notes. Sonny changed a thousand-frank note in order to pay the tab.

After that time Sonny began to drag Mak out to drink with him almost every evening. Every time Mak met with Sonny, even in his own house, Sonny would bring a bottle of wine without any hesitation, like before. He had obviously decided to make Mak his drinking partner. Mak behaves himself carefully during these drinking bouts, he is strong generally in relation to drink, and besides that – he would drink one wine glass and pour Sonny three.

Copied accurately

(Alekseev)

Bibliography

'Milaia moia resnichka'. Sergei Sedov. Pis'ma iz ssylki. Sbp: "Nits" Memorial; Hoover Institution Archives (Stanford University), 2006, p. 133. Online at http://www.sakharov-center.ru/asfcd/auth/?t=page&num=1481

"'...Ni razu ne govorilos' otnosiltel'no terror.' Stenogramma ochnoi stavki N.I. Bukharina s V.N. Astrovym v Politburo TsK VKP(b) 13 ianvaria 1937 g." *Istochnik* No. 2, 2001, 89-101.

"'Poslednii Polkovnik Imperii'" Interv'iu "Elementov" s narodnym deputatom SSSR Viktorom Alksnisom." *Elementy* No.3 (2000). Also at http://arctogaia.org.ru/modules.php?name=News&file=article&sid=423 (Alksnis)

"Het process te Moskou. Wie Niet Wil Bekennen Al Doodgeschoten? Trotski Jr. uit zijn opvatting." ("The Moscow Trial. Not all who want to confess are shot? Trotsky Jr. about its conception." *Het Volk*, Haarlem edition, January 28, 1937, p. 5.

"Interrogations of Nikolai Ezhov, former People's Commissar for Internal Affairs," at https://msuweb.montclair.edu/~furrg/research/ezhovinterrogs.html

"Ispoved' terrorista." *Voenno-Istoricheskii Arkhiv* No. 6 (2002), 25-59. About Jakov Bliumkin.

"Iz zala verkhovnogo suda SSSR. Zaiavlenie podsudimogo Evdokimova na sude 15 ianvaria sego goda." *Pravda* January 16, 1935, page 6, cols 5-6.

"Leon Trotsky: On the Kirov Assassination (December 1934)." At http://www.marxists.org/archive/trotsky/1934/12/kirov.htm

"O Tak Nazyvaemom 'Antisovetskom Ob'edinennom Trotskistsko-Zinov'evskom Tsentre." *Izvestiia TsK KPSS* 8 (1989), pp. 78-94.

"Pokazaniia Tukhachevskogo M.N. ot 1 iiunia 1937 goda." *Molodaia Gvardiia* 9 (1994), 129-136. (MG 9)

"Pokazaniia Tukhachevskogo M.N. ot 1 iiunia 1937 goda." *Molodaia Gvardiia* 10 (1994), 255-266. (MG 10)

"Protokol Doprosa IA.A. Iakovleva. 15-18 oktiabria 1937 g." *Lubianka 1937-1938* No. 226, pp. 387-395. At http://msuweb.montclair.edu/~furrg/research/iakovlev_conf_1037.pdf Posted without pagination at http://www.alexanderyakovlev.org/fond/issues-doc/62056/61208

"Rasskaz o desiati rasstreliannykh" ("Story of ten who were shot"), *Izvestiia* September 2, 1992, p. 3.

"Sedov et V. Serge devant la commission rogatoire." *Cahiers Léon Trotsky* No. 41 (July 1990), 80-114.

"Spravka Komissii Prezidiuma TsK KPSS 'O Proverke Obvinenii, Pred'iavlennykh v 1937 Godu Sudebnymi i Partiinymi Organami tt. Tukhachevskomu, Iakiru, Uborevichu i Drugim Voennym Deiateliam, v Izmene Rodiny, Terrore I Voennom Zagovore." In RKEB 2, 671- 788. (Spravka)

"Stenogramma ochnykh stavok v TsK VKP(b). Dekabr' 1936 goda. No. 3. Stenogramma ochnoi stavki mezhdu Piatakovym i Bukharinym v TsK VKP(b) ot 7 dekabria 1936 goda." *Voprosy Istorii* 4 (2003) 3-12.

"Stenogramma ochnykh stavok v TsK VKP(b). Dekabr' 1936 goda." *Voprosy Istoriii* No. 3, 2002.

"Telegramma L.D. Trotskogo v TsIK s osuzhdeniem politiki I.V. Stalina s rezoliutsiei I.V. Stalin I avtografami V. Molotova, K. Voroshilova. Na 3 ll. F.3, op.24,d.163, l.179-181." Volkogonov Archive, Library of Congress. At http://msuweb.montclair.edu/~furrg/research/trotsky_telegram061837.pdf

"Ustrialov, Nikolai Vasil'evich." (Biographical article). At
http://www.hrono.info/biograf/ustryalov.html

"Zapiska Komissii Prezidiuma TsK KPSS v Prezidium TsK KPSS of
Rezul'tatakh Raboty po Rassledovaniiu Prichin Repressiy I Ob-
stoiatel'stv Politicheskikh Protsessov 30-kh Godov." In RKEB 2,
541-670. (Zapiska)

Bazhanov, Boris. *Vospominaniia byvshego sekretaria Stalina*
("Memoirs of Stalin's former secretary"), Moscow, n.p. 1990. At
http://www.hrono.ru/libris/lib_b/bazhan00.html

Belton, John M., *The Commission of Inquiry Into Charges Made
Against Leon Trotsky in the Great Purge Trials in Moscow.* Emory
University, 1966.

Biulleten' Oppozitsii. 1929-1940. At
http://web.mit.edu/fjk/www/FI/BO/index.shtml and
http://www.1917.com/Marxism/Trotsky/BO/index.html

Bobrov, Vladimir L., "Taina smerti Ordzhonikidze," at
http://vif2ne.ru/nvz/forum/archive/238/238967.htm ;
fully footnoted Russian version at
http://msuweb.montclair.edu/~furrg/research/bobrov-
ordzhon08.html ; English translation at
http://msuweb.montclair.edu/~furrg/research/bobrov-
ordzhon08eng.html

Bobrov, Vladimir L'vovich. "Rasshifrovka audiozapisi besedy s
deputatom V.I. Alksnisom." Held on August 13, 2000 at the State
Duma of the Russian Federation. Typescript, 4 pp. (Bobrov)

Broué, Pierre. "Le GPU à la chasse aux trotskystes." *Cahiers Léon
Trotsky* 70 (2000), 89-98.

Broué, Pierre. "Compléments à un article sur les trotskystes en
U.R.S.S" *Cahiers Léon Trotsky* 24 (1985) 63-72.

Broué, Pierre. "L'historien devant la vie. Charles A. Beard et les
procès de Moscou." *Cahiers Léon Trotsky* 19 (1984), 68-77.

Broué, Pierre. "Party Opposition to Stalin (1930-1932) and the First Moscow Trial." In John W. Strong, ed. *Essays on Revolutionary Culture and Stalinism*. Columbus, OH: Slavica Publishers, 1990, pp. 98-111. (Broué, POS)

Broué, Pierre. "Trotsky et le bloc des oppositions de 1932." *Cahiers Léon Trotsky* 5 (Jan-Mar 1980), pp. 5-37. (Broué 1980)

Broué, Pierre. "Liova le 'fiston'." *Cahiers Léon Trotsky* 13 (1983), 5-24.

Broué, Pierre. *Léon Sedov. Fils de Trotsky, Victime de Staline*. Paris: Editions Ouvrières, 1993.

Broué, Pierre. *Trotsky*. Paris: Fayard, 1987.

Bystriantseva, L.A. "Arkhivnye materialy po N.V. Ustralovu (1890-1937)."
http://lib.irismedia.org/sait/lib_ru/lib.ru/politolog/ustryalov/documentation.txt.htm

Bystriantseva, L.A. "Ustremlenie k istine. Protokol doporosa N.V. Ustrialova." *Klio* (St. Petersburg) No. 1 (1999), 246-256.

Cahiers Léon Trotsky. (Institut Léon Trotsky. - Saint Martin d'Hères: Inst., 1979-2003). ISSN 0181-0790 (CahLT)

Chuev, Feliks I. *Kaganovich. Ispoved' stalinskogo apostola*. Moscow, 1992.

Chuev, Feliks I. *Kaganovich. Shepilov*. Moscow: OLMA-PRESS, 2001.

Chuev, Feliks I. *Molotov: Poluderzhavnyi Vlastelin*. Moscow: OLMA-PRESS, 1999.

Cohen, Stephen F. *Bukharin and the Bolshevik Revolution 1888-1938*. New York: Oxford University Press, 1973.

Cohen, Stephen. "Bukharin na Lubianke." *Svobodnaia Mysl'* 21, No. 3 (2003), 58-63.

Commission of inquiry into the charges made against Leon Trotsky in the Moscow trials. Preliminary Commission Coyoacán, Mexico, 1937. *The Case of Leon Trotsky. Report of hearings on the charges made against him in the Moscow trials.* By the Preliminary Commission of Inquiry: John Dewey, chairman [and others]. New York: Harper & Brothers, 1937. (CLT)

Conquest, Robert. *The Great Terror. A Reassessment.* 40th Anniversary Edition. New York: Oxford University Press, 2008.

Coox, Alvin D. "The Lesser of Two Hells: NKVD General G.S. Lyushkov's Defection to Japan, 1938-1945." *Journal of Slavic Military Studies* 11, 3 (1998) 145-186 (Part One) (Coox 1); 11, 4 (1998) 72-110 (Part Two).

Coox, Alvin D. "L'Affaire Lyushkov: Anatomy of a Defector." *Soviet Studies* 19, 3 (January 1968), 405-420.

Costello, John, and Oleg Tsarev. *Deadly Illusions.* NY: Crown, 1993.

Deutscher, Isaac. *The prophet outcast : Trotsky, 1929-1940.* London, New York : Oxford University Press, 1963.

Dimitrov, Georgi. *The diary of Georgi Dimitrov, 1933-1949.* Ed. Ivo Banac. New Haven : Yale University Press, 2003.

Egge, Osmund (Åsmund). *Zagadka Kirova. Ubiystvo, razviazavshee stalinskii terror.* Moscow: ROSSPEN, 2011.

Feferman, Anita Burdman. *Politics, logic, and love : the life of Jean Van Heijenoort.* Wellesley, Mass.: A K Peters, Ltd., 1993. (Feferman)

Fel'shtinskii, Iurii, Georgii Cherniavskii, *Lev Trotskii. Vrag No.1. 1929-1940.* Moscow: Tentrpoligraf, 2013.

Fel'shtinskii, Iurii. "Protest protiv publikatsiia pis'ma Trotskogo Fel'shtinskim i ego otvet." At http://lib.ru/HISTORY/FELSHTINSKY/f7.txt

Fel'shtinsky, Iurii. *Vozhdy v zakone.* Moscow, Terra, 1999.

Ferr, Grover (Furr). *Antistalinskaia Podlost'*. Moskva: Algoritm, 2007. (Antistalinskaia)

Frinovskii, M.P. ."... ot arestovannogo FRINOVSKOGO M.P. ZAIAV-LENIE." *Lubianka* 3 33-60. Russian original at https://msuweb.montclair.edu/~furrg/research/frinovskyru.html English translation at https://msuweb.montclair.edu/~furrg/research/frinovskyeng.ht ml

Furr Grover and Vladimir Bobrov, *1937. Pravosudie Stalina. Obzhalovaniiu ne podlezhit!* Moscow: Eksmo, 2010.

Furr, Grover and Vladimir L. Bobrov. "Stephen Cohen's Biography of Bukharin: A Study in the Falsehood of Khrushchev-Era 'Revelations.'" In Cultural Logic 2010. At http://clogic.eserver.org/2010/Furr.pdf (Furr and Bobrov Cohen)

Furr, Grover and Vladimir L. Bobrov. "Nikolai Bukharin's First Statement of Confession in the Lubianka." *Cultural Logic* 2007. At http://clogic.eserver.org/2007/Furr_Bobrov.pdf (Furr and Bobrov Bukharin)

Furr, Grover and Vladimir L. Bobrov. "Marshal S.M. Budyonny on the Tukhachevsky Trial. Impressions of an Eye-Witness" (in Russian). *Klio* No. 2 (2012), pp. 8-24.

Furr, Grover, and Vladimir L. Bobrov. "Bukharin's 'Last Plea': Yet Another Anti-Stalin Falsification." At http://msuweb.montclair.edu/~furrg/research/bukhlastplea.html

Furr, Grover. "(Un)critical Reading and the Discourse of Anti-communism." The Red Critique 11 (Spring 2006). At http://www.redcritique.org/WinterSpring2006/uncriticalreading andthediscourseofanticommunism.htm

Furr, Grover. "Evidence of Leon Trotsky's Collaboration with Germany and Japan." *Cultural Logic* (2009). At http://clogic.eserver.org/2009/Furr.pdf (Evidence)

Furr, Grover. "New Light On Old Stories About Marshal Tukhachevsky: Some Documents Reconsidered." *Russian History* 13, No. 2-3 (Summer-Fall 1986; actually published in 1988), 293-308. (Furr, New Light)

Furr, Grover. "Stalin and the Struggle for Democratic Reform" (two parts) in *Cultural Logic* (2005). At http://clogic.eserver.org/2005/furr.html and http://clogic.eserver.org/2005/furr2.html

Furr, Grover. "The Moscow Trials and the "Great Terror" of 1937-1938: What the Evidence Shows." At http://msuweb.montclair.edu/~furrg/research/trials_ezhovshchina_update0710.html

Furr, Grover. *Blood Lies. The Evidence that Every Accusation Against Joseph Stalin and the Soviet Union in Timothy Snyder's Bloodlands Is False.* New York: Red Star Publications, 2014. (Furr, Blood Lies)

Furr, Grover. *The Fraud of the Dewey Commission. Leon Trotsky's Lies.* New York: Red Star Publishers, 2018.

Furr, Grover. *Khrushchev Lied: The Evidence That Every "Revelation" of Stalin's (and Beria's) Crimes in Nikita Khrushchev's Infamous "Secret Speech" to the 20th Party Congress of the Communist Party of the Soviet Union on February 25, 1956, is Provably False.* Kettering, OH: Erythrós Press & Media LLC, 2011. (Furr, Khrushchev Lied)

Furr, Grover. *Leon Trotsky's Collaboration with Germany and Japan: Trotsky's Conspiracies of the 1930s, Volume Two.* Kettering, OH: Erythrós Press & Media, LLC, 2017.

Furr, Grover. *The Moscow Trials as Evidence.* New York: Red Star Publishers, 2018. (Furr, Moscow Trials)

Furr, Grover. *The Murder of Sergei Kirov. History, Scholarship and the Anti-Stalin Paradigm.* Kettering, OH: Erythrós Press and Media, LLC, 2013. (Kirov)

Furr, Grover. *Stalin: Waiting For ... The Truth! Exposing the False-hoods in Stephen Kotkin's Stalin. Waiting for Hitler, 1929-1941.* New York: Red Star Publishers, Corrected Edition April, 2019.

Furr, Grover. *Trotsky's "Amalgams": Trotsky's Lies, The Moscow Trials As Evidence, The Dewey Commission. Trotsky's Conspiracies of the 1930s, Volume One.* Kettering, OH: Erythrós Press & Media, LLC, 2015. (Furr Amalgams)

Genrikh Iagoda. Narkom vnutrennikh del SSSR, General'nyi komisar gosudarstvennoi bezopasnosti. Sbornik dokumentov. Kazan', 1997. (Genrikh Iagoda)

Getty, J. Arch. (Getti, Dz.A.) "Trotskii v izgnanii. Osnovania IV Internatsionala." *Voprosy Istorii KPSS* 5 (1991), 72-83.

Getty, J. Arch and Oleg V. Naumov. *The Road to Terror: Stalin and the Self-Destruction of the Bolsheviks, 1932-1939.* New Haven: Yale University Press, 1999. (Getty & Naumov)

Getty, J. Arch. "State and Society under Stalin: Constitutions and Elections in the 1930s." *Slavic Review* 50, 1 (Spring 1991), 18-35.

Getty, J. Arch. "Trotsky in Exile: the Founding of the Fourth Inter-national." *Soviet Studies* XXXVIII, no. 1 (January 1986), pp. 24-35. (TIE)

Getty, J. Arch. *Origins of the Great Purges: The Soviet Communist Party Reconsidered, 1933-1938.* New York and Cambridge: Cambridge University Press, 1985.

Getty, J. Arch. post to H-RUSSIA list Nov. 24 1998. At http://tinyurl.com/getty-trotsky-lied

Getty, J. Arch, and Oleg V. Naumov. *Yezhov : the rise of Stalin's "iron fist."* New Haven : Yale University Press, 2008.

Gould, Stephen Jay. "Dinosaurs in the Haystack" *Natural History* 101 (March 1992): 2-13. At http://www.inf.fu-berlin.de/lehre/SS05/efs/materials/Dinosaur-Leviathan.pdf

Harvard Trotsky Archive, Houghton Library, Harvard University. (TA)

Holmström, Sven-Eric. "New Evidence Concerning the 'Hotel Bristol' Question in the First Moscow Trial of 1936." *Cultural Logic* (2009). At http://clogic.eserver.org/2008/Holmstrom.pdf (Homström, New Evidence)

Humanité. Various issues, December 1934-January 1935.

Humbert-Droz, Jules. *Mémoirs de Jules Humbert-Droz. De Lénin à Staline, Dix Ans Au Service de L' Internationale Communiste 1921-31*. Neuchâtel: A la Baconnière, 1971. (Humbert-Droz)

Izvestiia TsK KPSS. (1989-1991).

Kantor, Iulia. Four articles in *Istoriia Gosudarstva i Prava* (2006). At http://msuweb.montclair.edu/~furrg/research/kantor_4articles_igp06.pdf (Kantor 2006)

Kantor, Iulia. *Voina i mir Mikhaila Tukhachevskogo*. Moscow: Izdatel'skii Dom *Ogoniok* "Vremia," 2005. (Kantor Voina)

Kantor, Iulia. Zakliataia druzhba. Sekretnoe sotrudnichestvo SSSR I Germania v 1920-1930-e gody. M-Spb: "Piter," 2009.

Khlevniuk,Oleg V. "Stalin, Syrtsov, Lominadze: Preparations for the 'Second Great Breakthrough.'" *The Lost Politburo Transcripts. From Collective Rule to Stalin's Dictatorship*. Ed. Paul R. Gregory and Norman Naimark. Stanford, CA: Hoover Institution (2008).

Khrushchev, Nikita S. The New Leader.The Crimes of the Stalin Era. Introduction by Anatol Shub, notes by Boris Nikolaevsky. New York: The New Leader, 1962.

Kirker, Harold and Burleigh Taylor Wilkins. "Beard, Becker and the Trotsky Inquiry." *American Quarterly* 13, No. 4 Winter 1961 pp. 516-525.

Larina, Anna. *Nezabyvaemoe*. Moscow: Izd-vo APN, 1989.

Larina, Anna. *This I cannot forget : the memoirs of Nikolai Bukharin's widow.* New York : W.W. Norton & Co., ©1993. (Larina)

Lenoe, Matthew. *The Kirov Murder and Soviet History* New Haven: Yale U.P. 2010. (Lenoe)

Léon Sedov, "La situation des bolcheviks-léninistes russes," *Cahiers Léon Trotsky* 24 (1985), 116-120.

Littlepage, John D. "Red Wreckers in Russia." *Saturday Evening Post* January 1, 1938, 10-11, 54-55.

Littlepage, John D. and Demaree Bess. *In Search of Soviet Gold.* New York: Harcourt, Brace, 1938. I have used the edition by George Harrap & Co. Ltd, London, 1939.

*Lubianka. Stalin i Glavnoe Upravlenie Gosbezopasnosti NKVD. 1937-1938.*M.: "Materik," 2004. (Lubianka 1937-1938)

Lubianka. Stalin i NKVD-NKGB-GUKR "Smersh." 1939 – mart 1946. Moscow: MDF, 2006 (Lubianka 1939-1946)

Lubianka. Stalin I VChK-GPU-OGPU-NIKVD. IAnvar' 1922 – dekabr' 1936. Moscow: IDF, 2003 (Lubianka 1922-1936)

Main, Steven J. "The Arrest and 'Testimony' of Marshal of the Soviet Union M.N. Tukhachevsky (May-June 1937)." *Journal of Slavic Military Studies* 10, No. 1 (March 1997), 151-195. (Main)

Marie, Jean-Jacques. *Trotsky. Révolutionnaire san frontières.* Paris: Payot & Rivages, 2006. (Marie, Trotsky)

McNeil, Robert H. "Trotsky's Interpretation of Stalin." Canadian Slavonic Papers 5 (1961) 87-97.

Medvedev R. A. *Let History Judge: The Origins and Consequences of Stalinism.* New York, 1971.

Not guilty: report of the Commission of Inquiry into the Charges Made Against Leon Trotsky in the Moscow Trials, John Dewey, chairman. New York, London, Harper & Brothers, 1938; 2nd edition New York, Monad Press, distributed by Pathfinder Press, 1973. (NG)

Obvinitelnye materialy po delu podpol'noi kontrrevolutsionnoi gruppy zinov'evtsev. Moscow: Partizdat TsK VKP(b), 1935.

Pétrement, Simone. *Simone Weil. A Life*. Translated from the French by Raymond Rosenthal. New York: Pantheon Books, 1976

Pfaff, Ivan. "Prag und der Fall Tuchatschewski." *Vierteljahreshefte für Zeitgeschichte* 35, 1 (1987), 95-134.

Politbiuro i Lev Trotskii. Tom 2. Ed. Oleg B. Mozokhin. Praha : Sociosféra-CZ, 2013. (PiLT2)

Poole, Thomas Ray. *"Counter-Trial." Leon Trotsky on the Soviet Purge Trials*. Unpublished Ph.D. dissertation, University of Massachusetts, 1974.

"Postanovlenie Plenuma Verkhovnogo Suda SSSR от 4 fevralia 1988 g." Volkogonov Archives, Library of Congress, Washington DC. (Postanovlenie 1988)

Protsess Bukharina 1938. Dokumenty. M: Mezhdunarodniy Fond „Demokratiia" i Fond Stivena Koena i Katriny Vanden Khiuvel, 2013.

Reabilitatsia: Politicheskie Protsessy 30-x - 50-x gg. Moscow, 1991. (R-PP)

Reabilitatsiia. Kak Eto Bylo. Febral' 1956 – nachalo 80-kh godov. T. 2. Moskva: "Materik," 2003. (RKEB 2)

Reabilitatsiia. Kak Eto Bylo. Seredina 80-kh godov – 1991. Dokumenty. T. 3. Moskva: "Materik," 2004. (RKEB 3)

Reabilitatsiia: Kak Eto Bylo. Mart 1953 – Fevral' 1956 gg. Dokumenty Prezidiuma TsK KPSS i Drugie Materialiy. Moskva: Mezhdunarodnyi Fond "Demokratiia," 2000. (RKEB 1)

Report of Court Proceedings in the Case of the Anti-Soviet "Bloc of Rights and Trotskyites" Heard Before the Military Collegium of the Supreme Court of the U.S.S.R. Moscow, March 2-13, 1938...Verbatim Report. Moscow: People's Commissariat of Justice of the U.S.S.R., 1938. (1938 Trial)

Report of Court Proceedings in the Case of the Anti-Soviet Trotskyite Centre. Heard Before the Military Collegium of the Supreme Court of the U.S.S.R. Moscow, January 23-30, 1937....Verbatim Report. Moscow: People's Commissariat of Justice of the U.S.S.R., 1937. (1937 Trial)

Report of Court Proceedings. The Case of the Trotskyite-Zinovievite Terrorist Center. Moscow: People's Commissariat of Justice of the U.S.S.R., 1936. (1936 Trial)

Rogovin, Vadim. "Prilozhenie I: Iz istorii razoblacheniia stalinskikh prestupleniy." *Partiia rasstreliannykh.* Also at http://web.mit.edu/people/fjk/Rogovin/volume5/

Rogovin, Vadim Z. *1937.* At http://trst.narod.ru/rogovin/t4/oglav.htm

Rogovin,Vadim Z. *1937. Stalin's Year of Terror.* Oak Park, MI: Mehring Books, 1998. (Rogovin 1937)

Sakharov, Valentin. A. "Podlog zaveshchaniia vozhdia. Kto avtor?" http://stalinism.narod.ru/vieux/saharov.htm

Sakharov,Valentin A. *"Politicheskoe zaveshchanie"V.I. Lenina: real'nost' istorii i mify politiki.* Moscow: Izdatel'stvo MGU [Moscow State University], 2003.

Sayers, Michael, and Albert E. Kahn, *The Great Conspiracy: The Secret War Against Soviet Russia.* Boston: Little, Brown & Company, 1946. (Sayers & Kahn)

Schwartz, Stephen. "Ante Ciliga (1898-1992): A Life at History's Crossroads." *Revolutionary History:* Unpublished Articles, 34, at https://web.archive.org/web/20010411013259/http://www.rev olutionary-history.co.uk/supplem.htm

Sedov, Leon. *Livre rouge sur le procès de Moscou.* Paris: Editions populaires, 1936. (Sedov, Livre rouge)

Sedov, Leon. *The Red Book on the Moscow Trials* (1936). At http://www.marxists.org/history/etol/writers/sedov/works/red/

Service, Robert. *Stalin: A Biography.* Harvard University Press, 2005). (Service, Stalin)

Sokolov, B.V. *Mikhail Tukhachevskii. Zhizn' I Smert' 'Krasnogo Marshala'.* Smolensk, 1999

The Diary of Georgi Dimitrov 1933-1949. Intro. & ed. Ivo Banac. New Haven: Yale University Press, 2003. (Dimitrov)

Izvestiia'TSK KPSS. Moscow: Izd. TSentral'nogo komiteta KPSS, Izd. TSentral'nogo komiteta KPSS, 1989-1991 (Izv TsK KPSS)

Thurston, Robert. *Life and Terror in Stalin's Russia, 1934–1941.* (Yale University Press; 1998).

Trotsky, Leon. "Pis'mo Trotskogo Zhene." Ed. Iurii Fel'shtinskii. At http://lib.ru/TROCKIJ/letter.txt

Tsarev, Oleg, and John Costello (Kostello). *Rokovye illiuzii: iz arkhivov KGB : delo Orlova, stalinskogo mastera Shpionazha.* Moscow: "Mezhdunarodnye otnosheniia," 1994.

Van Heijenoort, J. "The History of Trotsky's Papers." *Harvard Library Bulletin* July 1980: 291-298. (van Heijenoort History)

Van Heijenoort, Jean. *With Trotsky in Exile : from Prinkipo to Coyoactan.* Cambridge: Harvard University Press, 1978. (WTIE)

Viktorov, B.A. *Bez grifa «Sekretno». Zapiski voennogo prokurora.* Moscow: Iuridicheskaia Literatura, 1990. (Viktorov)

Voennie Arkhivy Rossii, 1993.

Volkogonov Papers, Library of Congress.

Writings of Leon Trotsky [1934-1935]. 2nd edition. New York: Pathfinder Press, 1974.

XXII s"ezd Kommunisticheskoi Partii Sovetskogo Soiuza. 17-31 oktiabria 1961 goda. Stenograficheskii otchiot. Moscow: Gos. Izd. Politicheskoi Literatury, 1962.

Zborowski archive, F.31660 d. 9067 Papka No. 28. In Volkogonov Archive, Library of Congress. At http://msuweb.montclair.edu/~furrg/research/zbor_sedov_stalin 0238.pdf

Zhukov, IU. *Inoi Stalin.* Moscow: Vagrius, 2003.

Zhukov, IU. *Stalin: Tainy Vlasti.* Moscow: Vagrius, 2005.

Zhukov, Iurii N. *Tainy Kremlia. Stalin, Molotov, Beriia, Malenkov.* Moscow: TERRA, 2000.

Index.

Made in the USA
Monee, IL
04 June 2024

59393475R00114